REFLECTIONS ON THEOLOGY AND GENDER

Fokkelien van Dijk-Hemmes
Athalya Brenner
(editors)

Reflections on Theology and Gender

Kok Pharos Publishing House
Kampen - the Netherlands

CIP-GEGEVENS KONINKLIJKE BIBLIOTHEEK, DEN HAAG

P.O. Box 5016, 8260 GA Kampen, The Netherlands
Cover Design By Rob Lucas
ISBN 90 390 0111 1
NUGI 632

CONTENTS

Preface

From september 1992 to march 1993 Athalya Brenner, Hebrew Bible and Women's Studies scholar from Haifa, Israel, was visiting professor at the Belle van Zuylen Chair at Utrecht University. On the occasion of her inaugural lecture a study day was organized by the 'Werkgroep Vrouwenstudies Theologie' (the Women's Studies work group in Theology). The aim of the study day was to present a first draft of a Women's Studies research program in the Faculty of Theology. This first step toward a Women Studies' research program in theology is one of the results of Professor Brenner's stay in Utrecht.

The papers read at the study day have been rewritten for publication in this volume and are presented here as the first fruit of, and an incentive for, further evolvement of the envisaged research program. We hope that, in addition to its primary target audience at the Utrecht Faculty of Theology, this collection of essays will be of interest to all those who query the so-called gender neutrality of theological research.

In Chapter 1, the Women's Studies research program is introduced by Dr. Fokkelien van Dijk-Hemmes, lecturer in Old Testament and Women's Studies at the Faculty of Theology in Utrecht University. The proposed structure of the program is designed to provide a measure of autonomy for Women's Studies while, at the same time, combining this autonomy with integration into the existing disciplinary programs of the Faculty.

Chapters 2 and 3 are examples of biblical research which fits into the proposed research program. Drs. Mieke Heijerman, who graduated in 1992, advances several portraits of the "strange" woman of Proverbs 7. Dr. Jan Willem van Henten, lecturer in New Testament at the Faculty of Theology in Utrecht (and now Professor of New Testament in the Faculty of Theology, University of Amsterdam), compares the book of Judith to the narratives about Moses and argues for a recognition of the presentation of Judith as a better Moses. In contrast to more orthodox modes of biblical criticism, both articles proceed from a reader-response perspective.

In Chapters 4 and 5 the proposed program is commented on by two involved "outsiders". Dr. Rosi Braidotti, Professor of Women's Studies at the Utrecht Faculty of Arts, cautions against the suggestion that "gender" and concepts relating to it are ideologically or socially neutral. In her opinion, in order to be effective this concept should be replaced by the adjective "feminist" or, alternatively, used as a verb. Dr. Anne-Marie Korte, lecturer in Women's Studies and Theology at the Utrecht Catholic University of Theology, views the research program from the perspective of recent developments in Women's Studies theological research at Dutch Universities.

Chapter 6 contains the text of Athalya Brenner's inaugural lecture.

Fokkelien van Dijk-Hemmes
Athalya Brenner

Toward a Women's Studies Research Program in the Faculty of Theology, Utrecht University

Fokkelien van Dijk-Hemmes

Once upon a time, research done at the university used to testify to the "most individual expression of the most individual interest" of a certain scholar. Nowadays this fairy-tale-like situation does not exist anymore. Instead, academic research has become a collective effort, a question of programs and of individual projects fitting into such programs. A grave disadvantage of this latter situation is, or at least can be, the amount of time it consumes. The deliberations and the negotiations required for the construction of a research program, as well as the repeated demand for reporting progress, take so much time that there is hardly any left for the research itself. Instead of doing research scholars continuously plan, discuss and write about the research that, according to them, should be done.

This somewhat exaggerated description of the state of affairs with regard to the organization of academic research applies, I think, especially to the first period of a new venture. Usually, new structures do not get established without growing pains. On the other hand, the obverse side of the coin has been demonstrated as well: a commitment to cooperate appears to entail the possibility of discussing, at least twice a year, methods of research and matters of content with one's colleagues. And that certainly constitutes an important advantage the new approach provides over and against the preceding individualistic era.

As to Women's Studies, that new and innovative offshoot of

academic disciplines, its arrival at the university scene broadly coincided with the introduction of the new research system. So in a sense we, the Women's Studies practitioners, do not know any better. From the very beginning our research was a collective and, as a matter of fact, an interdisciplinary effort. The first Interfacultary Women's Studies research program, which was developed and carried out in Utrecht from 1984 onwards, was named "Women between Control and Movement". It consisted of two parts: a cluster on "Labour and Care in Movement", developed by researchers from different disciplines within the Social Sciences; and a cluster on "Representation", done by researchers from the Faculties of Arts, Theology, Philosophy and Social Sciences. From 1990 on each cluster continued as an autonomous research program, the titles of which now turned into: "Gender, Morality and Care" for the Social Sciences program; and "Women: Text, Body, Power" for the Arts-, Theology-, and Philosophy program. To the latter a Natural Sciences and Social Pharmacy segment was added, with the title "Medicalisation of the Female Body: Especially of the Processes of Aging in Women".

Because participation in the Interfacultary Women's Studies Work Group, nowadays transformed into the Anna Maria van Schuurman Centre, forms part of my job, I was involved in the developments just described since 1985. I first participated in the "Representation" cluster and, subsequently, in the "Women: Text, Body, Power" program. Attendance of the research colloquia within those frameworks, which were started by Professor Rosi Braidotti, has been extremely stimulating for me. It was fascinating to work together with women from different disciplines. The discussions sometimes turned out to be a real Babel of tongues, but we experienced this as challenging more than discouraging. It was also a real challenge to present in such company the results of, or the questions asked within, theological research. Theologians, especially when they specialize in the Hebrew Bible, are considered strange animals within the field of Women's Studies. Nevertheless, we were always granted a listening ear to and a curious interest in our work. We, in turn, of course benefited greatly from other women's research and the methods used thereof. As far as I personally was concerned, the advantages I derived from the interdisciplinary programs relate first and foremost to the methods and theories developed within feminist literary criticism.

Given this state of affairs you might ask: Why start an autonomous Women's Studies program in the Faculty of Theology? Why not continue the cooperation with other disciplines which is, evidently, so fruitful? My answer to those questions is twofold.

1) The development of an autonomous Women's Studies/ Theology program does not necessarily imply an end to the cooperation with other disciplines. To a certain extent it unmistakably does imply that. Instead of attending the research colloquia of the Arts Faculty, I now give priority to the research colloquium started last year in our Faculty together with the KTU (Catholic Theological University of Utrecht). But, within the framework of the Anna Maria van Schuurman Centre, ways and means can undoubtedly be found for new models of collaboration. In fact, with respect to the finances allocated for research activities such as the organization of seminars and so on, priority is given to interdisciplinary projects like, for example, when the Law Faculty organizes a symposium together with the Faculty of Arts and/or with other Faculties.

2) My second answer to possible objections to an autonomous Women's Studies/Theology program is that theology itself consists of quite a number of different disciplines. Hence, the overt reduction to our own field in fact does not necessitate a farewell to interdisciplinarity, but, on the contrary, encompasses the latter. Enough reason, I think, to at least try to start a Women's Studies/ Theology Program, the first draft of which I'm going to present to you now.

1. *Gender and Theology*

The first part of the program's provisional title is "Gender and Theology". Until now, this part of the title has not been challenged, that is, it is unchallenged by the members of the research colloquium, where the proposed program has already been discussed twice. After Rosi Braidotti's paper, however, our opinions may have changed. Braidotti has announced her intention to present us with a serious attack on the concept of "gender". However, finding ourselves blissfully ignorant at this point, we can have an unsuspecting look at the concept itself and at its applications in theological research.

The application of "gender" to theology implies, first and foremost, the questioning of gender neutrality inside theology. It implies the recognition that theology is practised by gendered persons, mostly males, and that their being gendered probably affects their work. "Gender" refers to "the social construction and representation of differences between the sexes. It assumes that the subject is not universal in the sense of being sexually neutral but rather that he/she is sexed/genderized" ("Women: Text, Body, Power", Utrecht, 1989: 3).

On the basis of this definition we can say that research done under the banner of "Gender and Theology" takes the gendered situation of theology into account, and addresses itself to gender motivated reinterpretations of the texts and concepts which are used within the different disciplines of theology.

Moving on now to the second, disputed part of the title, I first give you four alternative proposals for a subtitle.

1) The Perspective of Submerged Women's Voices in Text, History, Community and Religious Traditions.

2) Representations of Feminine or other submerged Perspectives in Theological Texts and Religious Traditions.

3) Representations of Women's Realities in Text, History, Community and Religious Traditions.

4) Submerged Women's Perspectives in Text, History, Community and Religious Traditions.

As you can see, this part of the title is still under discussion. Let me immediately confess that I prefer the first subtitle, and would like to take advantage of this opportunity to explain why. For me as well as for Athalya Brenner, with whom I prepared the first draft of this research program, the concept of "voice" seems highly relevant.

The grammatical category of "voice" is, next to "gender", another term which feminism has appropriated from linguistics (and biology). In grammar "voice" refers to the mode of action reported: it indicates an "active" or a "passive" mode. When "gender" is borrowed into literary, or philosophical, or theological analyses, it is used as a metaphor for the speaker, the implicit or explicit "I" speaking in a text and the form in which this subject speaks. The concept of "voice" thus stimulates the person analysing a text to enquire who is speaking, whose view is presented and whose interests are at stake. In this research program the emphasis is actually on the uncovering of "submerged women's voices". Attention is drawn to strategies of marginalization: Who/what contributes to the marginalization, the rendering inaudible, of women's voices in past and present times? The uncovering and then recovery of "submerged women's voices" can, following Morton, be named as "hearing to speach" (1972: 39). The "hearing to speach" of a muted category of people requires adequate frames of reference, methods and concepts. The concept of "women's culture", developed within anthropology and adopted by literary and biblical scholars (Brenner and van Dijk-Hemmes 1993), has proven its usefulness in this respect. With the aid of the "women's culture" concept a distinction can be made between the roles, activities, preferences, and rules of behaviour prescribed for women and "those activities, patterns of behaviour and functions which arise from the life of women themselves" (Showalter 1986: 260). As "women's culture" mostly forms the invisible backdrop for a dominant culture, the application of this concept can point to the fact that the language spoken by women can often be characterized as "double voiced". A "muted" story can be detected alongside the "dominant" story. The "voice" is a loaded, polyvalent literary constellation.

2. *Structure*

After this passionate plea on behalf of the preservation of the "voice" concept in the title of our research program, and before presenting some examples of actual research projects, I now turn for a moment to the program's proposed structure. From the beautiful design — produced by Babs van den Bergh, the secretary of Integon (The Research Institute for Theology and Religious Studies) — you can see that what our program aims at is a combination of autonomy and integration.

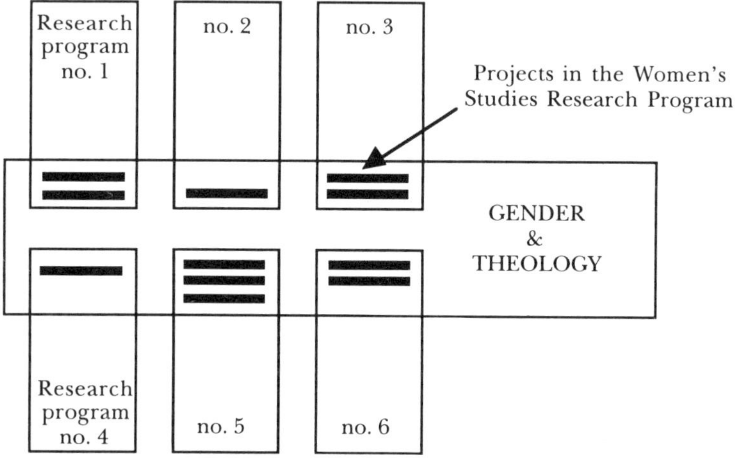

We consider it important that the distinctive features of research in Women's Studies/Theology be highlighted. The research done in this field in our Faculty has to become visible instead of being hidden away within so called gender-neutral research programs, or instead of being ousted to programs of other Faculties. But on the other hand this research should, at least for the time being, be integrated into the different research programs already functioning in our Faculty. Therefore we have opted for a so-called "cross-connection structure": The Women's Studies research projects in the Gender and Theology program will continue to constitute part of the existing, separate disciplinary programs. Research projects which deal with aspects of Women's Studies will only partially participate, insofar as is relevant, in the Gender and Theology program.

3. *Projects*

I will now present you with some examples of Women's Studies projects which are being drafted or developed within the framework of the different research programs in our Faculty.

— Within the program entitled "The Cultural Milieu of Early Christianity" two projects, or parts of projects, relate to Women's Studies:
1) The project of Mrs. Drs. Misset-van de Weg, and
2) the subproject of Mr. Dr. van Henten.
Since Dr. van Henten is going to present an example of his research project himself, I shall confine myself to the first project mentioned. Its title is, "Sarah and Thecla as Models of Faith: Meaning, Aim, and Backgrounds of 1 Peter 2:11-3:12 and the Acts of Thecla". Its aim is to contribute to our knowledge about women's situation in early Christian communities. As far as I can see the texts examined clearly illustrate how, by following the concept of "women's culture", a distinction can be made between the roles and rules of conduct prescribed for women (1 Peter); and the activities and desires which emanate from the lives of women themselves (Acts of Thecla).
— Within the Philosophy of Religion program, a project which is an explicitly Women's Studies project is being carried out by Mrs. Drs. Kosterman. The object of her research is a specific aspect of the language developed within the women's movement and feminist theology. She investigates which notions of justice and human well-being are at the foundation of the construction of alternative God-language (God-Talk, Ruether 1983) within Women's Studies/Theology.

— Within the program titled "Reconstruction and Interpretation of Religious Traditions", several projects are explicitly connected with Women's Studies. Mr. Achsa is preparing a publication on the position of women in Islam. A volume is being prepared by Professor Dr. R. Kloppenborg on "Stereotyped Women: (Re)Constructions and Reinterpretation of Women's Life Histories in Various Religious Traditions". Next to those, a project on "Religious Socialization of Surinam-Hindustan (Hindu) Girls of the Second Generation" has recently been started by Mrs. Drs. van den Bercken. She examines, by making use of the "double voice" concept, the connection between religion and the formation of the gender identity and the self-image of those girls.
— Two programs do not exhibit overt connections with Women's Studies, although, as far as I can see, there is every reason to develop such connections. The first is the "History of Protestantism, with Emphasis on Reformed Protestantism in the Netherlands". Here projects on the effects of this history upon women and on the contributions of women to this history could be developed. In the case of the second program, "Context and the Perception of Life", it is even more obvious that a gendered approach is required. The way people perceive their life and attribute meaning to it might have something to do with the gender they belong to. Investigation of "Aspects of Religious Education and the Socialization of Children and Young People" cannot be done in a gender-neutral way. It cannot be done as long as children are gendered beings, and as long as boys and girls are socialized differently. Therefore, negotiations about possibilities of collaboration with the "Gender and Theology" program have to be undertaken.
— Finally, something must be said about "The Early and Late Prophets" program of the Old Testament department of our Faculty. Women's Studies projects certainly can enhance this program. Part of my own proposed project, "The Marriage Metaphor in Prophetic Literature", fits into the Prophets program without any difficulty. However, the rest of my project exceeds the OT program's limits by dealing with texts other than prophetic ones. Those other parts of my project are a continuation of the quest for

F (Female/Feminine) and M (Male/Masculine) voices in the Hebrew Bible, and focus on the theme of sexuality. The project emanated from the course I gave together with Professor Brenner last autumn and will be continued together with her. The transgression of the OT program's prophetic boundaries will be indispensible for our project.

There certainly is a long way to go toward a Women's Studies research program at the Faculty of Theology in Utrecht. This is a fascinating and challenging enterprise. The first steps toward it have been taken now; we owe quite a lot to the stimulating and inspiring contribution of Athalya Brenner. The cooperation with her during her six-month Professorship was marvellous. By means of the new book we have just planned, our working relationship will continue. Its first fruit, *On Gendering Texts: Female and Male Voices in the Hebrew Bible*, is officially published today. We want to celebrate the public launching of the Women's Studies research program by offering a copy to the Dean of the Faculty of Theology, Prof. Dr. R. van den Broek.

Postscript

After discussing this paper in the Research Colloquium of Women's Studies/Theology, the following title for the research program has been chosen:

Gender and Theology: In Search of Women's Perspectives and Voices in Text, History, Community and Religious Traditions.

References

Bekkenkamp, Jonneke, Dröes, Freda, Korte, Anne-Marie (eds.), *Van zusters, meiden en vrouwen; Tien jaar feminisme en theologie op fakulteiten en hogescholen in Nederland,* IIMO Research Pamphlet; 19, Leiden/Utrecht, IIMO/IWFT, 1986.

Bekkenkamp, Jonneke, et al. (eds.), *Proeven van vrouwenstudies theologie,* I, IIMO Research Publication; 25, Leiden/Utrecht, IIMO/IWFT, 1991.

Bekkenkamp, Jonneke, et al. (eds.), *Proeven van vrouwenstudies theologie,* II, IIMO Research Publication; 32, Leiden/Utrecht, IIMO/IWFT, 1991.

Brenner, A. and F. van Dijk-Hemmes, *On Gendering Texts: Female and Male Voices in the Hebrew Bible,* Leiden, Brill, 1993.

Conceptvoorstel voor geprogrammeerd onderzoek Vrouwenstudies aan de Faculteit Godgeleerdheid RUU 1993–1997, *Gender and Theology: In Search of Women's Perspectives and Voices in Text, History, Community and Religious Traditions,* Utrecht, 1993.

Dijk-Hemmes, Fokkelien van, *Sporen van vrouwenteksten in de Hebreeuwse bijbel,* Utrechtse Theologische Reeks; 16, Utrecht, Faculteit der Godgeleerdheid, Universiteit van Utrecht, 1992.

Dröes, Freda, et al. (eds.), *Proeven van vrouwenstudies theologie,* III, IIMO Research Publication; 36, Leiden/Utrecht, IIMO/IWFT, 1993.

Korte, Anne-Marie, "Stromen en stremmingen. Structurele inbeddingen van het vrouwenstudies theologie onderzoek in Nederland", in Dröes, Freda, et al. (eds.), *Proeven van vrouwenstudies theologie,* III, IIMO Research Publication; 36, Leiden/Utrecht, IIMO/IWFT, 1993, 243–259.

Morton, N., "Preaching the Word", in A.L. Hageman (ed.), *Sexist Religion and Women in the Church,* New York, Association Press, 1972, 29-46.

Papavoine, Marian, "Feministisch-theologisch onderzoek in Nederland, 1986–1990", in Bekkenkamp, Jonneke, et al. (eds.), *Proeven van vrouwenstudies theologie,* II, IIMO Research Publication; 32, Leiden/Utrecht, IIMO/IWFT, 1989, 247–266.

Showalter, E. (ed.), *The New Feminist Criticism. Essays on Women, Literature and Theory*, London, Virago Press, 1986.

VF-Programma Vrouwenstudies aan de Faculteit Letteren RUU 1989–1993, *Women: Text, Body, Power*, Utrecht, 1989.

Who would blame her? The "strange" woman of Proverbs 7

MIEKE HEIJERMAN

I would like you to meet the "strange" woman of Proverbs 7. Is she really as strange as she is presented? Before I go further into the matter, I shall refresh your memories and recount briefly what is reported in Proverbs 7. In Proverbs 7 there is a speaker who instructs his or her son (vv. 1-2): it is not clear whether the speaker is a man or a woman. This speaker repeats again and again that her or his words are very important for the son: his life is at stake. If the son does not listen to these words but, instead, follows the smooth words of the "strange" woman, he will surely die. The speaker's self-claimed important words form a little exemplary story. This story, which I shall paraphrase in my own words, unfolds as follows.

Although it is dark, the speaker looks down through a window and sees a guy without a heart walking in the street. This guy runs across a woman who is dressed, we are told, like a harlot, a whore. According to the speaker she is restless and rebellious, unable to stay in her home. This "strange" and unknown woman seizes the guy and kisses him (vv. 6-13). Then she says — her words are reported by our textual speaker, of course — and I quote:

> Sacrifices are with me, and today I pay my vows;
> so now I have come out to meet you, to seek you eagerly,
> and I have found you.
> I have decked my couch with coverings,
> coloured spreads of Egyptian linen;
> I have perfumed my bed with myrrh, aloes, and cinnamon.
> Come, let us take our fill of love till morning;
> let us delight ourselves with love.
> For the man is not at home;

he has gone on a long journey;
he took the bag of money with him;
at the full moon he will come home.

(Prov. 7:14-20; Translation: RSV, modified by me.)

Then the speaker goes on to say that the guy listens to the "strange" woman, which will cost him his life. And the speaker repeats that the sons (now in the plural) have to listen to her or his words because otherwise the "strange" woman will lead them into the chambers of death.

1. *Questions and Responses to the Text*

When I first read this chapter of Proverbs, my primary response was one of defence. I thought, well, here we encounter yet another biblical male speaker who attacks a woman. Therefore, the questions I wanted to investigate were: Who is this "strange" woman? What does the text mean when, in v. 5, it labels the woman זרה ("strange"?) and נבריה ("unknown", or "foreign"?). Is she actually capable of killing young men? And last but not least, is it possible for women to cope with such a text where at least traces of misogyny are evident?

In order to answer these questions, I first have to sort out the socio-cultural context of Proverbs. I came to realize that the textual material in Proverbs reflects several different contexts; therefore, the texts must be interpreted differently for each underlying context. Chronological contexts point to textual origins stemming from different periods. Possible social contexts are the tribe (in which case quite old material is preserved); the family; the school; the corporation or professional guild. And the literary context of Proverbs as a whole and of the Hebrew Bible must be considered too. All these contexts are far from well-established in scholarly Bible discourse.

The uncertainty about the socio-cultural context(s) of Proverbs 7 is not necessarily a handicap. It grants me ample room for interpretation. For instance, the textual speaker's identity is not a given factor. That speaker could be a father, a mother, a teacher, a religous person, and so on. I am therefore able, gratefully albeit carefully, to make use of this interpretative room for manoeuvre. What if the speaker is a man, and what kind of a man could he be? Or: why should a woman, a mother, warn her son(s) in this hostile manner? Before I could work out these thoughts, I had to take several other steps towards a more direct confrontation with the "strange" woman.

Having concentrated on the context(s), my second step was to focus on the text by means of a detailed exegesis of Proverbs 7. The exegesis produced a lot of detailed information, far too much to reproduce here. But some of the information is striking; and I would like to share it with you.

It turns out that the "strange" woman is a very active woman, contrary to almost all the men in Proverbs 7, except for the speaker (if, indeed, the speaker is a man). The son(s) to whom the speaker delivers the warnings, the young guy who meets the "strange" woman and the dead men "penetrated" by the "strange" woman, are all passive.

On the other hand, the woman herself gets what she wants: the boys and, probably, their money too. The speaker feels powerless, otherwise why should the speaker repeatedly ask the son to listen? A powerful person would need to just say the word and, consequently, achieve obedience.

This conclusion really made me feel good and proud of this "strange" woman. I suppose that this is one of the reasons why the speaker only speaks to sons and not to daughters. The speaker paints a picture of the "strange" woman that is much too attractive. Is this perhaps why she is called זרה, because normal women are not supposed to behave in such an independent manner?

Anyway, the fact remains that the woman is accused of leading young men unto death. So if I want to be a good advocate, I have to bring into the reading more than my pride about her independence.

I therefore concentrated on the verses in which the "strange" woman has the position of an object or a subject. Among other things, it appears that she dòes give some information concerning her circumstances, a kind of reason why she wants the young guy without a heart in her bed. Namely, in the beginning and at the end of her reported speech (vv. 14-20) she, directly or indirectly, mentions the subject of "money" (in v. 14 and in v. 20). Is she perhaps in need of money? In the following interpretation you will find that the consequenses of her alleged need for money is taken seriously. In the meantime we must keep in mind that the "strange" woman's words reach us through the mouth of the speaker. Hence, we are never sure whether the speaker is quoting her correctly or not. But, as we shall soon see, there may be a solution for this problem.

After this second step — my own exegesis, some more traces of which you will find in the final stage of interpretation — I turned to some biblical scholars. Unfortunately, I must admit that many male commentators, just like the speaker-in-the-text of Proverbs 7, do not in fact listen to the "strange" woman's words. From the outset, they accept that the speaker-in-the-text is right. This is contrary to the position upheld by most of the female scholars who behave, and are conscious of behaving, as apparent advocates of sorts for the "strange" woman. And this interpretative gender split corresponds to my reading intentions.

When I started my investigation, the question was: Who is the "strange" woman? By now I have exegeted the text. I have already read the interpretations of others (especially Brenner 1993; Camp 1985, 1987, 1988; van Dijk-Hemmes 1993; Newsom 1989; Yee 1989). I am therefore fairly confident that it is possible to paint several alternative portraits of this "strange" woman of Proverbs 7. And it is not just "possible"; it would constitute an injustice to her and to the textual speaker if I drew only one single picture of this woman. I want to deal seriously with both the textual speaker *and* the "strange" woman. The issue of contexts, which was referred to earlier, is involved here as well. And something strange happens at this stage. I hope you enjoy yourselves because you are going to meet three "strange" women instead of just one such woman. Do not be alarmed: I am sure that they will not lead you unto death.

2. *The First Portrait: A Mothers' Rival*

I shall name the first woman "a mothers' rival". In this reading option, Proverbs 7 is read as an admonition from the viewpoint of a mother, or all mothers in Israel who warn their sons about seductive women. "Listen to me, son! Do not listen to this dangerous woman in the street". In her turn the "strange" woman, in her seductive (reported) speech, does not mention a mother as a possible rival. No, she only mentions "the man" to whom she seems to belong anyhow (vv. 19-20). According to her, when he is not at home everything is possible. She does not reckon with jealous mothers or other jealous women. It is rewarding to see that the mother inverts the patriarchial order, inverts the status quo, while she is intent on speaking on behalf of this same order. She wants her son to behave sensibly, neatly, and to behave like a man with a heart who knows what he wants. But in her speech no such men with a heart are present. As we have seen, all the men are passive and impotent, while the "strange" woman but also the speaking mother herself are active and potent. This is contrary to reality then.

We can speak of a "double voice" here — a concept well known to those who have read Fokkelien van Dijk-Hemmes's dissertation (1992). A good listener and, I think, particularly female listeners get a double message. "Strange" women are wicked because they are deadly for men. However, being a "strange" woman is exciting: you can go out and do what you want while disregarding restrictive conventions. But the dominant wish of the mother is that her son maintains an intimate relationship with Lady wisdom and have insight. The son has to call wisdom and insight respectively his sister and his relative (v. 4). In other words, the mother wants her son to maintain a non-sexual but close relationship with herself.

Well, taking all this into account, who is the "strange" woman? From the mother's point of view, she is the woman from outside the family, especially from outside the close mother-son relationship. She is neither selected, nor bought by the family of mother and son, for the son. On the contrary: she offers herself, she takes the initiative. By so behaving, she places herself in the margin of society and, therefore, can be easily identified with chaos. Chaos and death are almost synonymous, so it is not surprising that the mother thinks the "strange" woman leads unto death.

As mentioned before, the words זרה ("strange") and נבריה ("unknown", "foreign"; v. 5) have to be explained according to their particular context; they may mean "strange" but also "different", "unknown", "foreign", "Other", and even any combination of these meanings. In this context זרה might mean the woman who is a typical non-mother, who operates outside the family structures on which society is based. Therefore she is "strange", unknown insofar as the mother is concerned.

It may be that the mother calls the woman "strange" for another reason too. In order to warn her son effectively, the mother has to partly identify herself with the "strange" woman, by delivering the latter's strange words through her own mouth. It is as if the mother herself plays the harlot she describes for a moment. Perhaps she finds the courage to do so only by fabricating as vast a distance between the "strange" woman and herself as possible. She places herself upstairs behind a window, while the woman is downstairs in the street; moreover, the mother calls the woman "strange", "unknown". In that case "strange" here also denotes what it often does: she is not like me, and I am the norm.

The first portrait of the "strange" woman, then, shows a woman who, in the mother's opinion, has not adapted herself to a society that (as we know) is a patriarchal society. She is a threat to the future of the son and, therefore, also to the future and happiness of the mother. Whether the "strange" woman actually adapts herself to society or does not adjust will become apparent in her third portrait.

3. *Second Portrait: A Men's Scapegoat*

But let us now turn to the second portrait, which I label "a men's scapegoat". My point of departure for this portrait is the book of

Proverbs as a whole. Now the speaker-in-the-text is the final editor of Proverbs, who must have been a man, and who must have totally internalized the mother's words. This speaker too lives in a society for which family structures are essential (according to Claudia Camp [1985], the early postexilic period is the plausible chronological background). The speaker is affected by, I suppose, the well known whore-madonna complex. He thinks that there are only two sorts of woman, whores or madonnas, and no other women in between. Clearly, the deviant behaviour of the "strange" woman made him decide that she belongs to the whores. Her behaviour damages early postexilic Israelite society, which requires solid families in order to preserve land and capital and, of course, obtain offspring. He recommends that distance be maintained from the "strange" woman because of her attractiveness. The speaker calls her "strange" and "unknown" precisely because he wishes her to remain so. It is as if he proclaims: I have never met such a woman; I have never been a guy without a heart, unlike the guy in my story, who let himself be seduced. So, the speaker presents himself as a shining example. Another reason for his calling the woman "strange" is because she neither possesses nor explores the female skills and attributes which he, also the final editor of the Woman of Worth poem in Proverbs 31, respects. Thus, while the speaker does not want to be acquainted with the "strange" woman, he, at the same time, strongly fulminates against her words. This is suspicious. Hence, can we learn something about the "strange" woman from her own words? Can we somehow meet her as she "really" is? What kind of a portrait materializes when we listen seriously to her own words instead of to the probably misleading words of the speaker?

4. *Third Portrait: A Needy Woman*

I have tried to listen carefully to the "strange" woman's words, and the picture to emerge constitutes a third portrait. I called it "a needy woman". The "strange" woman (and by the way: she does not call herself "strange") must be a woman with problems, although I am not sure what exactly her problems are. She hopes that her religious vows can help her (v. 14), but she needs money to fulfill them. She does not possess that money. "The man" (האיש, v. 19) may be rich, but he controls the money and has taken the money bag with him (v. 20). Many women who have lived before and after her have embraced the same solution: occasional prostitution. Selling one's body might not have been all that strange for ancient Israelite women. They must have become used to regarding themselves and their bodies as chattel; after all, when they were still little girls, their family has already sold them to the family of their future husbands. We should not view the "strange" woman's problem, for which she made a religious vow, lightly. Prostitution, when it entailed adultery as well, was a grave sin which carried death penalty. Karel van der Toorn (1989) shows that childlessness was one of the causes for women to take such vows. Childlessness was often a reason for men to send their wives away, so that childless women did not have much to lose. If experience teaches that religious vows lead to children, or that the ensuing adultery does (because men, husbands can also be infertile), the choice is quickly made. From this perspective, then, the "strange" woman is not a woman who does not adapt herself to society. On the contrary. She is perforce flexible, and lives in the religious hope that her life will undergo a favourable shift. She does everything in her power to achieve this shift. Who would blame her for that?

5. *The Significance of a Text like Proverbs 7*

Now that we have come into contact with the "strange" woman, there is still an important issue to discuss, namely: What is the worth of this text which is, at the very least, a partly misogy~nic text for women readers? How can we cope with it? I would like to set out several alternatives.

One. If you, as a woman, still get depressed by chapter 7 of Proverbs, I would say, do not worry, because the text is not meant for you. The speaker addresses a son and sons. Therefore, daughters, plug your ears. You are neither supposed nor obliged to listen to these words. It is helpful to keep this in mind.

Two. When sons are taught "wisdom" about women, it is important for women's self-interest that they be well informed about the contents of these lessons. We have just heard what the messages of Proverbs 7 are. Women can respond by gathering women's wisdom for the sake of other women, for the sake of daughters who should be told about men and how some of them can lead you into the chambers of death. Women can also teach their sons that prostitutes are women who deserve our respect. This not only serves prostitutes and women in general, but is also pedagogically smart. Every parent knows that things that are forbidden are extra-specially attractive for children.

Three. Proverbs 7 can be read as a beautiful example of transference and projection. Matters of which the speaker is afraid can be displaced by transference outside himself — or herself — and projected onto the "strange" woman. The mother might be afraid of her own wish to be as independent and powerful as the "strange" woman, while the male speaker might deny his sexual desires by attacking women who are like the "strange" woman. For instance, we all know about the North American preachers who strongly pleaded the case for exclusive marital sex and so on whereas, in the meantime, they skilfully practised the opposite.

And last but not least, the "strange" woman teaches us that chaos and creativity are closely linked to one another. Because she is socially marginal, the "strange" woman is not as safeguarded as she might be within her marriage. By relinquishing the protective shelter of marriage, although for a limited period only, she can afford to do and say things that are normally unacceptable for prim-and-proper women. Suddenly she can go wherever she pleases and speak and behave the way she wants. Instead of being almost dead she writes, by her deviant behaviour, her own biography. The speaker in Proverbs 7, as well as the many disapproving interpreters, must have been unaware that on this point they in fact cooperated with her.

Postscript

When I read this paper, some members of the audience raised issues to which I wish to respond.

Bob Becking asked whether a fourth portrait of the "strange" woman can be drawn, a portrait of a foreign goddess (for example, Egyptian or Ugaritic). I have just painted three portraits. I have not considered whether the "strange" woman's figure originates in a foreign religion because I did not feel that the "strange" woman functions as a goddess in the text. But a reader who is interested in such matters will undoubtedly find such cognates. Furthermore, I think that goddesses (and gods) are a sort of projection too. A god/dess is an Other too (as women are for men?). I merely wanted to point out that the "strange" woman in Proverbs 7 is a projection: made by women (the first portrait), by men (the second portrait) and maybe also by me (the third and last portrait). In that sense, I have perhaps presented two or three (foreign) goddesses!

Athalya Brenner asked whether I could commit myself to one favourite portrait, and whether there was a portrait on which I worked with the greatest pleasure. To which I answer: Yes, the second one, because it is also a portrait of men. I like to describe men as I did in the second portrait. This is how I can get rid (partly, I must say) of my aggression towards men. In fact, it agrees with the way the textual mother in the first portrait makes men look powerless and impotent. Hence, I like the first portrait too.

It is a pity, but I do not like the "strange" woman herself as much as it may seem, to judge by the third portrait. In fact she is too religious for me, too positive, and not "strange" enough. It is a too harmonious picture of a woman who is doing the best she can. Maybe she is too much like parts of me. I tend to like people who behave more strangely and more freely.

References

Brenner, A. and F. van Dijk-Hemmes, *On Gendering Texts: Female and Male Voices in the Hebrew Bible*, Leiden, Brill, 1993.

Camp, C.V., *Wisdom and the Feminine in the Book of Proverbs*, Sheffield, Almond Press, 1985.

——, "Woman Wisdom as Root Metaphor: A Theological Consideration", in K.G. Hoglund et al. (eds.), *The Listening Heart: Essays in Wisdom and the Psalms in honour of Roland E. Murphy*, Sheffield, JSOT Press, 1987, 45-76.

——, "Wise and Strange: An Interpretation of the Female Imagery in Proverbs in Light of Trickster Mythology", *Semeia 42* (1988), 14-36.

Dijk-Hemmes, F. van, *Sporen van vrouwenteksten in de Hebreeuwse bijbel*, Utrecht, Utrecht University, 1992.

——, in *On Gendering Texts. Female and Male Voices in the Hebrew Bible*. See Brenner 1993.

Newsom, N.A., "Woman and the Discourse of Patriarchal Wisdom: A Study of Proverbs 1-9", in P. L. Day (ed.), *Gender and Difference in Ancient Israel*, Minneapolis, Fortress Press, 1989, 142-160.

Toorn, K. van der, "Female Prostitution in Payment of Vows in Ancient Israel", *Journal of Biblical Literature 108/2* (1989), 193-205.

Yee, G.A., "'I have Perfumed My Bed with Myrrh': The Foreign Woman ('iššazārā) in Proverbs 1-9", *JSOT* 43 (1989), 53-68.

Judith as a Female Moses: Judith 7-13 in the Light of Exodus 17; Numbers 20 and Deuteronomy 33:8-11*

Jan Willem van Henten

In 1986 Fokkelien van Dijk-Hemmes wrote an article in Dutch, "Gezegende onder de vrouwen: een moeder in Israël en een maagd in de kerk", in which she discusses three women in biblical literature who were called "blessed among women" (Luke 1:42): Deborah, Judith and Maria.[1] She considers the story of Judith a reproductive reception of Judges 4 and 5 on Deborah and Jael; and stresses the tendency to depict the woman who brings life to Israel by killing a man in more agreeable terms, i.e. more agreeable for men. She points to the fact that in Jdt. 13:18 men are blessing Judith: "And Ozias said to Judith, 'My daughter, the blessing of God Most High is upon you, you more than all other women on earth...'"[2] and writes: "De 'gezegende boven de vrouwen' is omgevormd tot een voor mannen aantrekkelijk ideaalbeeld. De gevaarlijke aspecten van de 'moeder van Israël' die door te doden leven geeft zijn in een veilig kader gezet."[3] I do not want to challenge the utilization of Judges 4 and 5 by the author of Judith,[4] nor the possibility that the picture of women was adapted

* I thank Professor Athalya Brenner for the stimulating and refreshing discussions during her stay at Utrecht University and for her very helpful comments on the draft of this paper.

[1] Van Dijk-Hemmes 1986.

[2] Unless indicated otherwise, the translations of verses from the Bible or from Judith are according to the New English Bible with the Apocrypha, Oxford Study Edition, New York 1976.

[3] Van Dijk-Hemmes 1986: 141.

[4] Cf. White 1989.

in later texts to masculine norms. As a matter of fact, there is a beautiful example of this phenomenon in the First Letter of Clement of Rome concerning Judith. In chapter 55 Clement points to pagan and Jewish examples of men and women who saved their country by an act of self-denial or self-sacrifice. He mentions Judith and Esther in this context of praise of the Christian nation — the pagan and Jewish examples are presented as the forerunners of Christian heroines. His reference to Judith in 55:3-5 begins as follows: "Many women who were empowered by the grace of God accomplished many manly deeds. Judith, the blessed, asked from the elders of the city permission to go to the camp of the foreigners, when the city was besieged" (55:3f.). This detail, that Judith had to ask for permission to leave Bethulia, runs contrary to the story, where Judith simply informs the elders that she will leave to fulfill her plan and does not even tell them what she has in mind (ch. 8). Nevertheless, I will try to demonstrate that the depiction of Judith in the story itself is not so satisfactory for men as Fokkelien van Dijk-Hemmes suggests; and that it is, in a way, even quite radical in depicting Judith as a female alternative for the greatest hero of Israel's prehistory, the man who lead Israel out of Egypt and gave it God's Tora, Moses.

1. *Gender in Judith*

There are some indications that the book of Judith, a Hellenistic Jewish writing, is unconventional from the perspective of gender relations. One of those indications is the genealogy of Judith, which is quite extensive and extraordinary and clearly fictitious (8:1). The genealogy starts with the name Merari and ends with the name Israel. Merari is a very rare name. In the Hebrew Bible there is only one Merari, the third son of Levi (Ex. 6:16). So the genealogy probably begins with a reference to the tribe of Levi and ends with the father of the twelve tribes. There are twelve names in the list, which is another indication of its fictitious character, as Athalya Brenner pointed out to me near the photocopy machine in the Theological Institute. The tenth and eleventh names, Salamiel and Sarasadae, form a well known combination (Num. 1:6; 2:12). They belong to the tribe of Simeon. Somehow the author presents Judith in this genealogy as the ideal Israelite woman who represents more than one tribe. The names point to Manasseh, Issachar and especially Simeon and Levi. Against this background the introduction of Judith's husband in 8:2 can only be a joke: "Her husband Manasseh, who belonged to her own tribe and clan...". There was no tribe! Moreover, the husband derives his identity from his wife, not the other way around. If we compare this to other heroines in Hellenistic Jewish literature the difference is striking. Esther, for example, is called the daughter of Mordecai's uncle (Est. 2:7), the daughter of Abihail (2:15). She has no genealogy of her own, but Mordecai has one in 2:5. Esther's family is indicated through Mordecai. According to the Septuagint Esther is the daughter of Aminadab, but this name is probably a symbolic reference to Mordecai. It means, "The brother of my father is generous". So Esther derives her identity from Mordecai, which fits in with the unfolding of the story. It is Mordecai who persuades Esther in the end to go the Persian king in order to rescue her people (ch. 4).

The example of Esther draws our attention, by contrast, to another characteristic of Judith's story. It is Judith who takes the initiative in an independent way. After the decision of the elders to turn over the city to the Assyrians if after five days God has not intervened, Judith invites them into the shelter on the roof of her house (probably a *sukkah*)[5] and teaches them a lesson (8:9-36): "Listen to me, magistrates of Bethulia. You had no right to speak as you did to the people today, and to bind yourselves by oath before God to surrender the town to our enemies..." (8:11). They do not protest against the sharp reproaches of Judith, but suggest to her to pray for rain (8:31).[6] Judith ignores the request of the elders: "'Hear what I have to say', replied Judith. 'I am going to do a deed which will be remembered among our people for all generations... But do not try to find out my plan; I will not tell you

[5] Cf. Neh. 8:14-17.
[6] See for the background of this issue below.

until I have accomplished what I mean to do'" (8:32-34). The visit ends as follows: "Ozias and the magistrates said to her, 'Go with our blessing, and may God be with you to take vengeance on our enemies'" (8:35).[7] They leave the roof shelter and return to their posts. Thus, Judith manages to get a carte blanche from the magistrates.

A third indication seems to be a departure from the traditional pattern of men who act as warriors and liberators and women who sing the song of victory (Ex. 15:20f.; Jud. 11:34; 1 Sam. 18:6f.).[8] For instance, 1 Sam. 18:6f. reads: "At the home-coming of the army, when David returned from the slaughter of the Philistines, the women came out from all the cities of Israel to look on, and the dancers came out to meet King Saul with tambourines, singing, and dancing. The women as they made merry sang to one another: 'Saul made havoc among thousands but David among tens of thousands'". In the book of Judith the picture is quite different. As a matter of fact, Judith and her maidservant rescue the Jews from the siege. After the killing of Holophernes the battle of the Jews and the Assyrians is a piece of cake, and the author takes less then a chapter to describe it (14:11-15:7). In 16:1-17 we find an extensive song of triumph, started by Judith and joined by the rest of the people (15:14). The overture to this song in 15:8-13 is very interesting, compared to the songs of victory just mentioned. It looks like an inversion of gender roles. First Joakim the high priest and the senate come from Jerusalem to Bethulia "to see for themselves the great things the Lord had done for his people, and to meet Judith and wish her well" (15:8). They acknowledge that it was Judith who rescued Israel (15:9f.; cf. v. 10: "With your own hand you have done all this, you have restored the fortunes of Israel, and God has shown his approval"). Vv. 12f. refer to the dancing and singing of all women from Israel, and the men join

---

7 Jdt. 8:35 probably hints at the seduction of Holophernes, which is depicted as an analogy to the revenge of the rape of Dinah by Simeon and Levi (Gen. 34) in 9:2-4.

8 Goitein 1988. Van Dijk-Hemmes 1992: 81-92. Brenner & Van Dijk-Hemmes 1993: 32-43.

the party. I cannot go into detail now, but this again stresses the point that Judith is the heroine: "They sang her praises, and some of them performed a dance in her honour". At the conclusion of this section we can say that in the book of Judith we meet female singers and dancers *and* female liberators, and with one or two exceptions only foolish men.

2. *Judith 7-13 in the light of Ex. 17; Num. 20 and Deut. 33:8-11*

Several Hellenistic Jewish writings are closely linked to biblical literature, and in some of those we find not only biblical vocabulary, style and motifs, but also large parts of the narrative which are inspired by biblical passages. This probably holds true for the stories in the Greek Additions to Daniel (Susanna, Bel and the Snake)[9] and for Judith. In the remaining part of this paper I will try to convince you that Jdt. 7-13 is a remake of passages from Ex. 17, Num. 20 and Deut. 33.[10] My first step in doing this is a quick brainwash. Almost all scholars who study Judith assume a strong caesura between chs. 1-7 (or 4-7) and 8-16,[11] seduced as they are by the attractive figure of Judith, who is introduced in ch. 8 and functions as the central character in chs. 8-16. From a literary point of view, however, this assumption is less than satisfactory. There are several links between the terminology of chs. 7 and 8, and motifs introduced in ch. 7 are still important from ch. 8 onwards. There is strong evidence for the cohesion of chs. 7 and 8, which means that ch. 7 supplies the context for Judith's performance.

The outline of the book of Judith is similar to that of 1 and 2 Maccabees and the book of Esther. All these writings are "histories" of a pagan threat to the existence of Israel, and the rescue of

9 See for example Van Henten 1990 and Wesselius 1990.

10 Of course, other biblical passages are utilized as well; see Haag 1963, Craven 1983, Merideth 1989 and White 1989. But the thread of the narrative in chs. 7-13 seems to be inspired chiefly by Ex. 17, Num. 20 and Deut. 33: 8-11.

11 According to Craven 1983 and many other scholars, the book of Judith consists of two parts (I: chs. 1-7 and II: chs. 8-16). Haag 1963, however, connects ch. 8 with chs. 1-7 (I: chs. 1-8, and II: chs. 9-16). Weimar 1973: 131f. and Zenger 1981: 432f. advocate a composition in three parts (I: chs. 1-3; II: chs. 4-7; and III: chs. 8-16). See Zenger 1988: 405.

the people by ideal figures.[12] The saviours of Israel and the pagan aggressors are presented as opposing characters. Against the pitch-black description of the evil deeds of Antiochus IV in 1 Macc. 1, the actions of the Maccabean liberators appear in a very favourable light.[13] Holophernes's attack on the Jews is malicious. He carries out the plan of the generals of the nations which surround Israel, who have joined his army, and takes possession of the spring near Bethulia (7:6-18), so that the Jews would die of water shortage (7:7, 12, 17, 20f.). As every reader of Judith knows, the death of this aggressor is unique. Moreover, it connects with the attack through the motif of drinking. Holophernes dies during the aftermath of a drinking-bout (12:10, πότος), which he had organized to seduce Judith (12:1-13:2). While the Jews had no water to drink, he drank too much wine in anticipation of a night with Judith, and was like putty in her hands: "Holophernes was delighted with her, and drank a great deal of wine, more, indeed, than he had ever drunk on any single day since he was born" (12:20). And after the servants had withdrawn: "Judith was left alone in the tent, with Holophernes lying sprawled on his bed, dead drunk" (13:2).[14] The water and drinking motif is present from ch. 7 up to 13:2[15] and indicates, alongside other arguments, that chapters 7-13 should be regarded as a unity.[16]

This observation is confirmed by a chronological framework which starts in ch. 7 and ends in ch. 13, when Judith returns to Bethulia with the head of Holophernes in her knapsack. The events in ch. 7 to ch. 13 take exactly forty days,[17] so that Holophernes's threat to the Jewish nation may be associated with the

---

[12] Martola 1984, Van Henten 1989.

[13] According to 1 Macc. the actions of Antiochus IV and his men, and those of the Maccabees, are clearly opposites. The actions of both parties are described in three clusters, see Martola 1984.

[14] The drinking motif occurs time and again in 12:10-13:2; see 12:11, 13, 17-20 and 13:1-2. Cf. also 12:1, 7, 9.

[15] Cf. also 8:9, 30f.; 11:12. The drinking-bout (πότος) of Ozias, the elders and Achior in 6:21 probably anticipates this motif in chs. 7-13.

[16] Cf. the repetition of the feast motif in Esther; see Berg 1979: 31-47.

[17] Cf. 8:4: Judith is a widow for three years and four months (= 40 months).

exodus from Egypt. 7:1 contains a chronological marker with "on the next day". On this day Holophernes starts the war on the Israelites. On the second day (7:6f.) he, together with his cavalry, inspects the approaches to Bethulia and its springs, and decides to cut the Jews off from their water supply as the commanders of the Edomites, Moabites and the people from the coastal region suggest: "... let your servants take possession of the spring at the foot of the hill, for that is where all the townspeople of Bethulia get their water. When they are dying of thirst they will surrender the town" (7:12f.). After a siege of thirty four days (7:20), the inhabitants of the town are in great distress and urge the elders to surrender Bethulia. The elders decide to wait for another five days to see if God would rescue the people and, in case his help fails to materialize, surrender the town to the Assyrians: "Ozias said to them, 'Courage, my friends! Let us hold out for five more days; by that time the Lord our God may show us his mercy again. Surely he will not finally desert us. But if by the end of that time no help has reached us, then I will do what you ask'" (7:30f.). If we add up all the "days" mentioned in ch. 7, we get a total of forty days. Moreover, the decisive last five days of this scenario are described in chs. 8-13 (cf. 8:33). Judith hears[18] of the oath of Ozias and invites him and two other elders to come to her house in order to explain to them that they had taken a wrong decision. After a prayer (ch. 9), she makes preparations for her audacious plan and leaves Bethulia on the night of the 36th day. 12:7 informs us that Judith stays in the camp of Holophernes for three days, i.e. days 37 to 39. The *grand finale*, the drinking-bout, takes place on Judith's fourth day in the camp which is, according to the schedule, the 40th day: "On the fourth day Holophernes arranged a drinking-bout[19]

---

[18] Cf. the repetition of the verb ἀκούω in 8:1, 9 which forms an inclusio of the introduction of Judith; 8:1: "And in those days Judith heard" (NEB: "News of what was happening reached Judith"); 8:9: "When Judith heard of the shameful attack which the people had made upon Ozias the magistrate, because they were demoralized by the shortage of water..."). This shows again that Judith's acts should be seen as a reaction to the conduct of the people and the elders in ch. 7.

[19] NEB: "gave a banquet".

for his personal servants only..." (12:10). He dies on the night of that same fortieth day, and Judith and her maid return to Bethulia on that very night (13:11-20).

Because of the forty days framework, one is inclined to compare the Assyrian threat to the Jews in Judith with Israel's forty years in the desert after the flight from Egypt. Several details support this association. The situation of the starving Jews of Bethulia, who blame their leaders for not giving in to Holophernes, is similar to that of Israel that complains against Moses and Aaron and hankers after the fleshpots of Egypt. In 7:25 the inhabitants of Bethulia, lacking in faith, say: "Now we have no one to help us. God has sold us into their power; they will find us dead of thirst, and the ground strewn with our corpses". Even more reminiscent of the narrative of the exodus is 7:27: "It is better for us to be taken prisoner; for even as *slaves* we shall be alive, and shall not have to watch our *babies* dying before our eyes, and our wives and children at their last gasp". This thread of the narrative is resumed in Judith's speech to the elders in 8:11-34. Judith challenges the people's and elders' reaction to the shortage of water and links it to the testing motif (πειράζω). First she says that the elders were wrong to put God in a spot, because humans cannot know his decisions. In this connection, she blames them for putting God to the test: "Who are you to test God (οἳ ἐπειράσατε τὸν θεὸν) at a time like this, and openly set yourselves above him? You are putting the Lord Almighty to the proof. You will never understand!" (8:12f.). In the subsequent part of the speech Judith returns to this motif, but in a different way. She represents to the elders the probability that God would try his people by the lack of water: "We have every reason to give thanks to the Lord our God; he is putting us to the test (ὃς πειράζει ἡμᾶς) as he did our ancestors. Remember how he dealt with Abraham and how he tested Isaac (ὅσα ἐπείρασεν τὸν Ισαακ), and what happened to Jacob in Syrian Mesopotamia when he was working as a shepherd for his uncle Laban" (8:25f.). It is clear to Judith that the policy of the elders is wrong but, since they are bound by their oath, she decides to offer help within the five days of the oath (7:30f.; 8:30, 33).

After these indications of some links between ch. 7 on the one hand and chs. 8-13 on the other, I hope that you are convinced that we should combine ch. 7 with the performance of Judith, because this is decisive for my thesis, which I will try to unfold now. The point of departure for Judith's action seems to be the shortage of water in Bethulia. The three motifs just mentioned i.e. the water/drinking motif, the chronological framework of forty days, and the testing can be taken together as a reference to the exodus from Egypt, or to specific events during this period. In that case we are tempted to look for additional passages in the Tora which the narrative of Judith might echo. It is not difficult to find such passages, because only one episode contains the combination of the testing motif and a situation of lack of water: the scene in the desert at Massah and Meribah,[20] which is narrated twice in the Tora (Ex. 17:1-7; Num. 20:2-13) and taken up again in the "blessing" to Levi in Deut. 33:8-11.[21]

According to Ex. 17 Israel travelled from the desert of Sin to Rephidim, where it had to cope with a shortage of water (Ex. 17:1). The people start complaining to Moses that they are afraid of perishing and that they should have stayed in Egypt. These themes link up with ch. 16, where the Lord gives the heavenly bread of manna to the Israelites in the desert of Sin, because they have complained to Moses and Aaron that they had had plenty of bread in Egypt and wanted to return to the fleshpots. Ex. 16:4 already contains the testing motif: "The Lord said to Moses, 'I will rain down bread from heaven for you. Each day the people shall go out and gather a day's supply, so that I can put them to the test[22] and see whether they follow my instructions or not". The structure and several details of the short passage in Ex. 17:1-7

---

[20] The name Massah is connected with the root נסה, which occurs in Ex. 17:2, 7 (LXX πειράζω); the name Meribah with the root ריב, which occurs in Ex. 17:2, 7 (LXX λοιδορέω). Cf. the root לין in 17:3 (LXX γογγύζω) and also the episode at Marah in Ex. 15:22-26 with the bitter water (the testing motif occurs in 15:25 with נסה/πειράζω).

[21] There are several references to this episode in other biblical books, see for instance Deut. 8:15f. and Ps. 78:15-20. Cf. also Wisd. Sol. 11:4-9.

[22] MT: למען אנסנו; LXX: ὅπως πειράσω αὐτούς.

correspond quite closely to parts of the much larger narrative in Jdt. 7-13:[23]

1. Same point of departure, no water	Jdt. 7	Ex. 17:1
2. The people complain to the elders/ to Moses: Give us water; it is better to be a slave [in Egypt] than to die with [women], children [and cattle]	Jdt. 7:23-32 (Jdt. 7:27	Ex. 17:2f. Ex. 17:3)
3. The reaction of Judith/Moses (Judith criticizes the elders, who put God to the test, 8:12; on the contrary, it is the Lord who puts them to the test, 8:25f.; Moses asks the people: "Why do you put the Lord to the test?")	Jdt. 8:9-36	Ex. 17:2
4. Judith/Moses calls upon the Lord (prayer)	Jdt. 9	Ex. 17:4
5. Judith seduces Holophernes (which can be associated with adultery, cf. Jdt. 13:16, and with stoning as usual punishment [Deut. 22:22-27]/ Moses' exclamation of fear, "In a moment they will be stoning me"	Jdt.10-13	Ex. 17:4
(Judith leaves Bethulia with festive clothes and make-up, accompanied by her maid with a knapsack/ Moses goes forward ahead of the people, with some of the elders and his staff)	Jdt. 10	Ex. 17:5
6. Judith receives support from the Lord when she kills Holophernes/the Lord is with Moses at the rock	Jdt. 13:1-10	Ex. 17:6

[23] Incidentally, if these suggestions are defensible, we have a nice parallel to a linking of the story of Susanna to Jer. 29:21-23 too. The plot and the successive acts in Sus. correspond quite well to the few verses on the adultery and execution of the false prophets in Jer. 29. However, a lot of research still needs to be done in that direction. Cf. Van Henten 1990 and Wesselius 1990.

(Judith chops off the head of Holophernes; Moses strikes the rock)	Jdt. 13:4-8	Ex. 17:6
7. Similar conclusion: "The Lord is with us"	Jdt. 13:11-20	Ex. 17:7[24]

It is clear that the author of Judith did not simply fall back onto Ex. 17:1-7 for the construction of his own story in Jdt. 7-13. Several details of Jdt. 7-13 have no correspondences in Ex. 17, but seem to echo phrases in Num. 20:2-13 and Deut. 33:8-11. Judith strikes the neck of Holophernes twice with all her might (13:8), like Moses strikes the rock twice with his staff according to Num. 20:11. The remark about Judith's praying to the Lord at the time when the evening incense offering (τὸ θυμίαμα τῆς ἑσπέρας ἐκείνης) was being offered in the Jerusalem temple (9:1) echoes Deut. 33:10, where Moses indicates that the Levites shall offer the incense offering (LXX: ἐπιθήσουσιν θυμίαμα).[25] Judith's success is also better understood in the light of Moses' blessing to Levi in Deut. 33:8-11. The blessing seems to indicate a special position for the Levites within Israel, who enjoy the blessing of the Lord: "Bless all his power, O Lord, and accept the work of his hands (ברך יהוה חילו ופעל ידיו תרצה; εὐλόγησον, κύριε, τὴν ἰσχὺν αὐτοῦ καὶ τὰ ἔργα τῶν χειρῶν αὐτοῦ δέξαι). Strike his adversaries hip and thigh, and may his enemies rise no more" (33:11). Judith seems to refer to this blessing in her prayer and during the final scene: "Give in my hand, the hand of a widow, the power to achieve what I have in mind" (δὸς ἐν χειρί μου τῆς χήρας ὃ διενοήθην κράτος, 9:9); after she has grasped the hair of Holophernes she says: "Give me strength, O Lord..." (κραταίωσόν με, κύριε, 13:7). Some verses earlier she asks if God would look in this hour favourably on the work of her

[24] After her successful action Judith called: "God, our God, is with us" (μεθ' ἡμῶν ὁ θεὸς ὁ θεὸς ἡμῶν, 13:11). Hence the question of Ex. 17:7, "Is the Lord in our midst or not?" (LXX: εἰ ἔστιν κύριος ἐν ἡμῖν ἢ οὔ;), which dominates chs. 7-13, is answered positively at the end.

[25] As the echoes to Dt. 33:8-11 show (see below), Judith is especially affiliated to the tribe of Levi. Cf. also Merari as the first name in her genealogy and the reference to the revenge of the shameful act of Shechem with Dinah by Simeon and Levi in Jdt. 9:2-4. Cf. also 8:24 and 9:12.

hands (ἐπίβλεψον...ἐπὶ τὰ ἔργα τῶν χειρῶν μου) in order to bring glory to Jerusalem (13:4). We find another reference to her strength in the verse in which she chops off the head of Holophernes (ἐν τῇ ἰσχύει αὐτῆς, 13:8).[26] The blessing of Judith by Ozias in 13:18 (εὐλογητὴ σύ, θύγατερ, τῷ θεῷ τῷ ὑψίστῳ) is probably another echo of the blessing to Levi by Moses in Deut. 33:11,[27] indicating that her success should be understood as the handiwork of a daughter of Levi who is blessed by the Lord like Levi.[28]

Hence, the story in Jdt. 7-13 seems to be a creative and harmonizing combination of the three passages in the Tora concerning the episode at Massah and Meribah. The basic characters seem to be partly derived from Ex. 17, Num. 20 and Deut. 33. These are the people, the Lord, and the leaders. Apart from the elders, the leaders are named individuals: Moses in Ex. 17, Moses and Aaron in Num. 20, Levi/Moses in Deut. 33:8-11 (33:8 refers to the episode of Massah and Meribah explicitly); and Judith.[29] Throughout Jdt.

---

26 Cf. also 9:10; 13:15f. and 16:6.

27 Other possible echoes of Deut. 33:8-11 in Jdt. are Judith's piety, cf. Jdt. 8:5, 8, 31 with Deut. 33:8, concerning Levi (לאיש חסידך; LXX: τῷ ἀνδρὶ τῷ ὁσίῳ), and 33:9. Cf. Judith's wisdom (σοφία) and sagacity (σύνεσις, 8:29). Judith announces that she will speak reliable words to Holophernes (ῥήματα ἀληθείας, 10:13; cf. 10:16 and 11:5), which appears to be true and untrue at the same time. Cf. Levi's אורים and תמים in Deut. 33:8 (rendered by δῆλοι καὶ ἀλήθεια in the LXX). For the striking of Judith's adversaries by the Lord, so that they rise no more, cf. Deut. 33:11, מחץ מתנים קמיו ומשנאיו מן־יקומון, "strike his (i.e. Levi's) adversaries hip and thigh, and may his enemies rise no more" (LXX: κάταξον ὀσφὺν ἐχθρῶν ἐπανεστηκότων αὐτῷ καὶ οἱ μισοῦντες αὐτὸν μὴ ἀναστήτωσαν); and Jdt. 9:8 (κάταξον τὸ κράτος αὐτῶν) and 13:5 (εἰς θραῦσμα ἐχθρῶν, οἳ ἐπανέστησαν ἡμῖν). Cf. also Jdt. 13:11, 14, 17f.; 16:17.

28 Cf. the references to Deut. 33:8-11 by Taxo and his seven sons, who are also Levites, in Assumptio Mosis 9, see Van Henten 1987 and Tromp 1992: 223-227.

29 The correspondences suggested in this paper leave only one possibility for the identification of Holophernes, who has to be the rock of Ex. 17. My thesis need not be rejected at the outset because of this element. The versatility of the story of Judith should not be underestimated. Cf. the double entendre of several statements of Judith to Holophernes in ch. 11, which can be read as references to Holophernes himself, but also to God. See further Craven 1983. The identification Holophernes/rock might be derived from the Hebrew text of Ex. 17:6 by an *'al tiqre* exegesis: read אַשּׁוּר "Assur" for הַצּוּר "the rock" (Holophernes is commander in chief of the Assyrian army).

8, Judith's criticism of the elders' conduct as leaders is emphasized. It is interesting in this respect to compare the motif of the putting to the test (נסה; πειράζω) in these four texts. Who exactly puts whom to the test? In Ex. 17:2, 7 it is the people who challenge the Lord. In Num. 20 an explicit reference to this motif is absent, but the acts of Moses seem to imply that Moses is somehow put to the test. The MT of Deut. 33:8 clearly states that God put Levi, i.e. Moses, to the test at Massah. But the Septuagint has it differently: the people tested Moses.[30] In Judith several possibilities are combined. Judith criticizes the elders who, together with the people, put the Lord to the test (8:12); in reality, however, things are just the other way around: God tests the elders and the people (8:25-27). In addition to this we could ask whether chs. 9-13 suggest that Judith herself is tested in the camp of Holophernes. We could read these chapters as an echo of Deut. 33:8, with a reference to the testing of Levi/ Moses at Massah and Meribah. Let me remind you of the motif of drinking, which is present in the book of Judith up to and inclusive of the drinking-bout in ch. 13.

The correspondences between Ex. 17, Num. 20, Deut. 33:8-11 and Jdt. 7-13 enable us to compare the role of Judith, granddaughter of Levi according to Jdt. 8:1, with that of Moses, another descendant of Levi (Ex. 2:1).[31] This comparison is clearly advantageous for Judith. Let me point out some details. According to Ex. 17:4 Moses is afraid and cries to the Lord: "What shall I do with this people? In a moment they will be stoning me". Judith accomplishes her mission without complaining and never loses her self-control, either with the elders or with Holophernes. Moses does not know what to do and turns to the Lord in despair. Judith takes the initiative and realizes her plan, which is supported by the Lord. In Num. 20 Moses' behaviour gives sound reasons for criticism and, in the context of the book of Numbers, the punishment for this conduct is that Moses is not allowed to enter the promised land (Num. 20:12). Num. 20:7-11 describes how the

---

30 Ex. 17:2, מה־תנסון את־יהוה; 17:7, ועל נסתם את־יהוה. Deut. 33:8, נסיתו במסה; LXX: ὃν (Λευι) ἐπείρασαν αὐτὸν ἐν πείρᾳ.

31 Siebert-Hommes 1993.

impatient Moses disobeys the command of the Lord and strikes the rock with his staff: "...He (Moses) said to them, 'Listen to me, you rebels. Must we get water out of this rock for you?' Moses raised his hand and struck the rock twice with his staff." By comparison to this passage, Judith's obedience to the Lord is striking. She never gives in to the advances of Holophernes and keeps Jewish dietary laws while in the camp of the enemy.[32] Moreover, Judith attributes all credit for the rescue of the people to the Lord, see for instance 13:11: "From a distance Judith called to the sentries at the gates [of Bethulia]: 'Open! Open the gate! God, our God, is with us, still showing his strength in Israel and his might against our enemies. He has shown it today!'"

Therefore, could you perhaps consider the idea of Judith as a better Moses? I do not mind if you do not believe a word of what I have said. Indeed, my analysis is sheer fiction, just like the story of Judith.

Postscript

After presenting this paper Athalya Brenner pointed out that in my final remark to the audience I in fact referred to the (im)-plausibility of my reconstruction of the author's intent. Interpreting a text, she stated, does not necessarily entail the recovery of the meaning the author had in mind. Rather, interpretation is a question of a more or less convincing reader's response to a text. The same goes for the adaptation of an intertextual reading mode: it is the reader who connects different texts, and who recognizes and interprets the relations between them.

Therefore, I should perhaps rephrase my last sentence as follows: Therefore, could you perhaps consider the idea of Judith as a better Moses? This is the outcome of my reader's response to the text. It is up to you readers, to decide whether you consider it a more or a less convincing (or, maybe, interesting or complementary) portrait of Judith — more so than the comments by, for instance, Toni Craven or Fokkelien van Dijk-Hemmes.

---

[32] Cf. Dan. 1 and the prayer of Esther in LXXEst. 4:17k-z/C12-30.

Bibliography

Berg, S.B., *The Book of Esther: Motifs, Themes and Structure,* SBLDS 44, Missoula 1979.

Brenner, A. and F. van Dijk-Hemmes, *On Gendering Texts. Female and Male Voices in the Hebrew Bible,* Biblical Interpretation Series 1, Leiden 1993.

Craven, T., *Artistry and Faith in the Book of Judith,* SBLDS 70, Chico 1983.

Dijk-Hemmes, F. van, Gezegende onder de vrouwen: een moeder in Israël en een maagd in de kerk, in: *'t Is kwaad gerucht, als zij niet binnen blijft. Vrouwen in oude culturen,* Tekst en Maatschappij, Utrecht 1986, 123-147.

——, *Sporen van vrouwenteksten in de Hebreeuwse bijbel,* Utrechtse Theologische Reeks 16, Utrecht 1992.

Goitein, S.D., Women as Creators of Biblical Genres, *Prooftexts* 8 (1988), 1-33.

Haag, E., *Studien zum Buche Judith. Seine theologische Bedeutung und literarische Eigenart,* Trierer Theologische Studien 16, Trier 1963.

Henten, J.W. van, Traditie en interpretatie in TestMos 9:1-10:10, *Summa.* Blad van de Theologische Faculteit van de Universiteit van Amsterdam 19 (1987), 18-29.

——, Das jüdische Selbstverständnis in den ältesten Martyrien, in: J.W. van Henten et al. (eds.), *Die Entstehung der jüdischen Martyrologie,* Studia Post-Biblica 38, Leiden 1989, 127-161.

——, The Story of Susanna as a Pre-Rabbinic Midrash to Dan. 1:1-2, in: A. Kuyt, E.G.L. Schrijver & N.A. van Uchelen, *Variety of Forms. Dutch Studies in Midrash,* Publications of the Juda Palache Institute 5, Amsterdam 1990, 1-14.

Martola, N., *Capture and Liberation. A Study in the Composition of the First Book of Maccabees,* Acta Academiae Aboensis Ser. A 63 nr. 1, Åbo 1984.

Merideth, B., Desire and Danger: The Drama of Betrayal in Judges and Judith, in: M. Bal (ed.), *Anti-Covenant. Counter-Reading Women's Lives in the Hebrew Bible,* Journal for the Study of the Old Testament Supplement Series 81, Sheffield 1989, 63-78.

Siebert-Hommes, J., *Laat de dochters léven! De literaire architectuur van Exodus 1 en 2 als toegang tot de interpretatie*, Kampen 1993.

Tromp, J., *The Assumption of Moses. A Critical Edition with Commentary*, Leiden 1992.

Weimar, P., Formen frühjüdischer Literatur. Eine Skizze, in: J. Maier & J. Schreiner (eds.), *Literatur und Religion des Frühjudentums. Eine Einführung*, Würzburg-Gütersloh 1973, 123-162.

Wesselius, J.W., The Literary Genre of the Story of Susanna and its Original Language, in: A. Kuyt, E.G.L. Schrijver & N.A. van Uchelen, *Variety of Forms. Dutch Studies in Midrash*, Publications of the Juda Palache Institute 5, Amsterdam 1990, 15-25.

White, S.A., In the Steps of Jael and Deborah: Judith as Heroine, in: D. Lull (ed.), *Society of Biblical Literature Seminar Papers 1989*, Atlanta 1989, 570-578. Reprinted in: J.C. VanderKam (ed.), *"No One Spoke Ill of Her." Essays on Judith*, SBLEJL 2, Atlanta 1992, 5-16.

Zenger, E., Das Buch Judit, in: W.G. Kümmel & H. Lichtenberger (eds.), *Jüdische Schriften aus hellenistisch-römischer Zeit* I:6, Gütersloh 1981, 427-534.

——, Judith/Judithbuch, in: G. Müller et al. (eds.), *Theologische Realenzyklopädie* 17, Berlin/New York 1988, 404-408.

What's wrong with Gender?

Rosi Braidotti

In this paper I will first present an overview of contemporary feminist theory, especially in relation to the question of female subjectivity. Then I will analyze more specifically the notion of "gender", whose limitations for feminism I will attempt to spell out; I will then go on to outline what I see as the conceptual crisis of gender theories, and conclude by highlighting recent developments in feminist thinking about this notion.

1. *The Crisis of "Gender" as Theory and Practice*

My starting point is that the notion of "gender" is at a crisis-point in feminist theory and practice and that it is undergoing intense criticism, both for its theoretical inadequacy and for its politically amorphous and unfocussed nature. The areas from whence the most pertinent criticism of "gender" has emerged are: the post-colonial and black feminist theorists; the feminist epistemologists working in the natural sciences, especially biology, the sexual difference theorists and the lesbian theorists. I will come back to these areas of criticism and expand on them later.

A second remark. The crisis of gender as a useful category in feminist analysis is simultaneous with a re-shuffling of theoretical positions which had become fixed and stale-mated in feminist theory, most notably the opposition between on the one hand "gender theorists" in the Anglo-American tradition and on the other, "sexual difference theorists" in the French and continental tradition.[1] The debate between these two camps had become stuck

[1] See Claire Duchen 1986.

in the 1980's in a fairly sterile polemic between opposing cultural and theoretical frameworks which rest on different assumptions about political practice.[2] This polarized climate was reshuffled partly because of the increasing awareness of the culture-specific forms undertaken by feminist theory. This resulted in a new and more productive approach to differences in feminist positions.

A third related phenomenon in this respect is the recent emergence in the inter-national debate of Italian feminist thought as an alternative that helps split asunder the comfortably binary opposition between French Continental and Anglo-American positions.[3] These publications have contributed not only to putting another, however "minor" European feminist culture on the map, but also to stress the extent to which the notion of "gender" is a vicissitude of the English language, which bears little or no relevance to theoretical traditions in the Romance languages.[4] As such, it has found no successful echo in the French, Spanish or Italian feminist movements. If you think that in French "le genre" can be used to refer to humanity as a whole ("le genre humain"), you will get an idea of the culture-specific nature of the term and consequently also of its untranslatability.

This also means that the famous sex/gender distinction, which is one of the pillars on which English-speaking feminist theory is built, makes neither epistemological nor political sense in many non-English, western European contexts, where the notions of "sexuality" and "sexual difference" make much more sense. Although much ink has been spilled to either praise or attack theories of sexual difference, little effort has been made to try and situate the respective debates in their cultural contexts. In such a context I must welcome whole-heartedly the recent publication of a book-length study on the philosophy of sexual difference of Luce

---

2 For an attempt to by-pass the polemics and highlight the theoretical differences, allow me to refer you to my study: *Patterns of Dissonance* (1991).

3 See the Milan Women's Bookshop's collective effort, *Sexual Difference* (1990); also Bono and Kemp (eds.) 1991.

4 This point is strongly made by T. de Lauretis 1988: 3-37; see also the issue of *Les cahiers du Grif* devoted to women's studies: 45 (1990), "Savoir et différence des sexes".

Irigaray, by Margaret Whitford (1991), a book which introduces this complex thought with great subtlety, critical acumen and sensitivity.

The fourth and final remark I would like to make about "gender" concerns the institutional practice to which it gives rise, which turned out to be problematic for feminists. The scientific-sounding term "gender" appears to strike a more re-assuring note in the academic world than the more explicitly political: "feminist" studies. This factor is partly responsible for the success encountered by "gender studies" in universities and publishing houses. In my opinion, this success has resulted in a shift of focus away from the feminist agenda towards a more generalized attention being paid to the social construction of differences between the sexes. It is a broadening out which is also a thinning down of the political stakes.

Claiming that men have a gender too, many institutions have started to establish "men's studies" courses as a counter-part to and very often an alternative to women's studies. Although the male critiques of masculinity are extremely important and necessary, I think that this institutional competition between the broadening out of "gender studies" and the keeping up of the feminist agenda is regrettable.

This situation has led feminists to view "gender" as a bankrupt notion at the level of institutional practice.

2. *The Problem of Definitions*

The term "gender", as Haraway (1990) points out, is opaque in its very structure, partly because it is not a feminist idea: it rather has a long history prior to being taken up by feminist theorists, especially in biology and linguistics. When it was adopted into feminism it gained in complexity, rather than clarity.

A brief genealogical overview of "gender" in a feminist perspective is necessary because of the rich and complex theoretical history of the term. Recent feminist scholarship, especially in the humanities, has subjected the notion of "gender" to serious methodological and theoretical revisions.[5] The need has emerged to submit to critical scrutiny the central notions, the ruling concepts, the criteria for interpretation and evaluation, and the methodological frameworks that sustain and govern the production of feminist knowledge, thereby advancing also the claim that women's studies has produced its own epistemological categories.[6] Considering the intrinsic polysemy of the term "gender", it is not surprising that recent publications have attempted to define it in a feminist perspective, either by historicizing the notion or by setting it in a narrative framework: this is the option preferred by Snitow (1991) and Gallop (1991). See also the trend towards "personal criticism" in Miller (1991), Jouve-Ward (1991) and others. You can set these attempts at clarification of the opaque term "gender" alongside more epistemological works that try to analyze the implications of the term as a set of relations that allow us to think of the inter-dependence of gender and other variables of oppression such as race, age, culture, life-style and others, such as Scott's work.[7]

Therefore, for the sake of precision I would define "gender" as a notion that offers a set of frameworks within which feminist theory has explained the social and discursive construction and representation of differences between the sexes. As such, "gender" in feminist theory fulfils primarily the function of challenging the universalistic tendency of critical language and of the systems of knowledge and scientific discourse at large.

This tendency consists of conflating the masculine viewpoint with the general, "human" standpoint, thereby confining the feminine to the structural position of "other". Thus, the masculine *qua* human is taken as the "norm" and the feminine *qua* other is

---

[5] See Harding 1986, 1987; de Lauretis 1990: 115-150; Haraway 1990; Butler 1991; Braidotti 1991.

[6] Special mention should be made here of the case of feminist historians, who have managed to reach a high level of meta-discursive elaboration about their practice. Significant in this respect is the recent publication, in several European languages, of a multi-volume *Women's History*, edited by M. Perrot and G. Duby.

[7] Scott 1988: 33-50; 1990.

seen as marking the "difference". The corollary of this definition is that the mark of sexual difference falls upon women, marking them off as the second sex, or the structural "other", whereas men are marked by the imperative of carrying the universal.

The symbolic division of labour between the sexes, which the term "gender" helps to explain, is the system set up by phallo-logocentrism, which is the inner logic of patriarchy. In other words, this system is neither necessary as historically inevitable, nor is it rational as conceptually necessary. It simply *is*, as the powerful foundations of a system in which we are all constructed as either men or women by certain symbolic, semiotic and material conditions.

In such a system, the masculine and the feminine are in a structurally dissymetrical position: men, as the empirical referents of the masculine do not have a gender because they are expected to carry the Phallus, i.e.: to uphold the view of abstract virility, which is hardly an easy task. The central terms of reference for the debate on gender were fixed by feminist theory in the early 1970's, under the inspiration of S. de Beauvoir's work and mostly in fields such as history, anthropology and sociology.[8] S. de Beauvoir observed fifty years ago that the price men pay for representing the universal is a kind of loss of embodiment; the price women pay, on the other hand, is a loss of subjectivity and the confinement to the body. The former are disembodied and through this process gain entitlement to transcendance and subjectivity, the latter are over-embodied and thereby consigned to immanence. They result in two very dissymetrical positions and two opposed problem-areas.

By emphasizing the cultural and social construction of differences between the sexes, De Beauvoir's analysis highlights the importance of human sexuality as a location of power. She also singles out the institutions of the family and of procreative heterosexuality as major sites of regulation and power over sexual identity.

---

8 One of the classics here is G. Rubin's study in Rapp (ed.) 1975.

The critique of heterosexuality as a regulatory and normative institution is precisely the main direction taken by gender theories following Beauvoir. According to the account of the notion of "gender" provided by Donna Haraway (1990), the work of radical women like Gayle Rubin in anthropology, and feminist writers like Adrienne Rich radicalize Beauvoir's insight and turn the analysis of the normative role of heterosexuality into a political platform.

To expand on Rich's thought: The two central notions in her work are "the politics of location" and "the lesbian continuum". Both ideas are related to the notion that the feminist standpoint is marked by a specific location in space and time. The primary location is the female body, i.e.: the morphological and political space of the female embodied subject. Rich has the merit of emphasizing both the positivity of the difference that women embody and also of stressing the many differences that separate women among themselves, first and foremost among them, the differences of race and ethnicity. The commonness of a culturally-determined position that unites women as "the second sex" is consequently crossed over by powerful variables that are axes of difference: the issue of embodiment as the grounding of female subjectivity is therefore not a one-way road towards an essentialized female entity, but rather a bio-cultural situation.

With regard to Rich's "woman-based" knowledge, radical thinkers like Monique Wittig opposed the idea of the "lesbian continuum" by developing a critique of the very notion of "woman". In her polemical opposition to the valorization of sexual difference, Wittig argued that this notion is a constant factor of the male imaginary and of a social system that is dominated by men. As such, this notion is politically contaminated and theoretically useless because it encloses women in an essentialistic trap. Wittig proposes as an alternative the category of "lesbian", meant as a political positioning beyond the parameters of the male imaginary: it is therefore a position outside the patriarchally enforced dichotomous opposition of male and female. The lesbian is a sort of third sex, which Wittig also opposes to the glorification of the "feminine" in the thought of Hélène Cixous, Luce Irigaray and other theoreticians of radical sexual difference.

This approach, however, shifted in the early 1980's under the joint impact of semiotics, structuralist psychoanalysis and autonomous developments within the women's movement.[9] Central to this new approach is a shift away from the mere critique of patriarchy, to the assertion of the positivity of women's cultural traditions and range of experiences; the work of A. Rich (1976, 1979, 1985) is extremely influential in this respect, though mention should also be made of C. Gilligan (1982).

Of great importance for this shift of perspective is the new emphasis and value placed on language and consequently representation as the site of constitution of the subject. One of the most striking forms of this new development in feminist scholarship are the French theories of "sexual difference", also known as the "écriture féminine" movement. The conceptual foundations of this movement are drawn from linguistics, literary studies, semiotics, philosophy and psychoanalytic theories of the subject. The sexual difference theorists[10] innovated the feminist debate by drawing attention to the social relevance of the theoretical and linguistic structures of the differences between the sexes. They claimed that the social field is coextensive with relations of power and knowledge, i.e.: that it is an intersecting web of symbolic and material structures.[11] In other words, this school of feminist thought argues that an adequate analysis of women's oppression must take into account both language and materialism, and not be reduced to either one. They are very critical of the notion of "gender" as being unduly focused on social and material factors, to the detriment of the semiotic and symbolic aspects.

The debate between sexual difference and gender theorists in the 1980's resulted in two quite comparable forms of reductivism: on the one hand an idealistic form that reduces everything to the

---

9 For accounts of this shift of perspectives, see Duchen 1986 and also Eisenstein 1984.

10 See Irigaray 1974, 1977, 1984; also Cixous 1974, 1975, 1986, 1987.

11 As Foucault argues (1977).

textual, and on the other hand a materialistic one that reduces everything to the social. These led to two extreme versions of "essentialism".[12]

It seems to me that, beyond the polemic, one of the points of real, that is to say conceptual difference between the two camps is in the question of how to identify points of exit from the universalism implicit in the patriarchal or "phallo-logocentric" system and from the binary way of thinking that characterizes it. Whereas sexual difference theorists argued for the process of working through the old system, through the strategy of "mimetic repetition", gender theorists resorted to the "critique of ideology". This resulted respectively in the investment of the "feminine" pole of the sexual dichotomy in order to create different meanings and representations for it. On the other hand, it led to the rejection of the scheme of sexual bi-polarisation, in favour of a de-sexualized and gender-free position. In other words, we come to opposing claims: the argument that one needs to redefine the female feminist subject, which is reiterated by sexual difference theorists, is echoed by the contradictory claim of gender theorists, that the feminine is a morass of metaphysical nonsense and that one is better off rejecting it altogether, in favour of a new androgyny. Not surprisingly, these positions also imply quite different theoretical understandings of female sexuality in general and of female homosexuality in particular.[13]

What strikes me, however, as a fundamental point of consensus between the two is the idea that feminist practice, and women's studies with it, must challenge the universalistic stance of scientific discourse by attacking its inherent dualism. The rejection of dualistic thinking as the way of being of patriarchy provides the grounds for the unblocking of otherwise extremely opposed positions. Feminist scholars right across the board have

---

[12] For a discussion of essentialism, see: de Lauretis 1988; Schor 1988; Fuss 1990; Braidotti in Brennan (ed.) 1989; and Braidotti in Wright (ed.), forthcoming.

[13] One just has to compare the vision of female homosexuality in H. Cixous (1987) with that of M. Wittig (1973) to appreciate the difference.

been arguing that the universalistic stance, with the conflation of the masculine to represent the human and the confinement of the feminine to a secondary position of devalued "otherness", rests upon a classical system of dualistic oppositions, such as, for instance: nature/culture, active/passive, rational/irrational, masculine/feminine. Feminists argue that this dualistic mode of thinking creates binary differences only to ordain them in a hierarchical scale of power-relations. It is further claimed that this conceptual scheme had served the purpose of comforting western culture in its belief in the "natural", that is to say historically inevitable structure of its system of representation, its myths, symbols and the dominant vision of the subject which it contains.

It is against this background that in the 1990's a shift in position has occurred, which I see as a re-mixing of the previously opposed positions of sexual difference versus gender theorists. Symptomatic of this change in intellectual climate is the position recently taken by Joan Scott. As the author of one of the most authoritative early essays on the question of gender, Scott had argued that "gender" as marking a set of inter-relations between variables of oppression could help us understand the intersection of sex, class, race, life-style, age as fundamental axes of differentiation. In a more recent essay, Scott (1988: 33-50) goes further and argues for a definition of gender as marking the intersection of language with the social, i.e.: the semiotic with the material. Quoting Foucault's notion of "discourse", which she defends as one of the major contributions of poststructuralist thought to feminist theory,[14] Scott suggests that we re-interpret "gender" as linking the text to reality, the symbolic to the material, theory to practice in a new powerful manner. In Scott's reading, feminist theory in this post-gender phase politicizes the struggle over meaning and representation.

What emerges here is a radical redefinition of the text and of the textual away from the dualistic mode; the text is now

[14] This point has been the object of my book-length study (Braidotti 1991). See also Miller in de Lauretis (ed.) 1986 and N. Schor 1987.

approached as both a semiotic and a material structure, that is to say not an isolated item locked in a dualistic opposition to a social context and to an activity of interpretation. The text must rather be understood as a term in a process, that is to say a chain-reaction which encompasses a web of power-relations. What is at stake in the textual practice, therefore, is less the activity of interpretation than that of decoding the network of connections and effects that link the text to an entire socio-symbolic system. In other words, we are faced here with a new materialist theory of the text and of textual practice.

My central hypothesis in proposing such a reading of the notion of "gender" is that the gender theorists of today are a new trans-disciplinary and trans-national generation of thinkers, solidly anchored in the humanities, philosophy, social sciences, anthropology, history, semiotics and literary studies. People like de Lauretis (1987), Haraway, Butler (1991) are multi-layered thinkers who transcend disciplinary boundaries. They have been cross-influenced by different theoretical traditions and are less likely to take misnomers such as "French feminism" for granted, mostly because they have their share of false polemics generated by poststructuralism and its feminist adaptations.

3. *The New Gender Theorists*

In other words, the gender theorists of the 1990's have been exposed to the impact of theories of difference and have moved beyond them in a non-productive manner. I would distinguish the following groupings within this new generation ;

(a) The feminist critical theorists in the German tradition, united in their attachment to the Frankfurt tradition: Benhabib (1987), Benjamin (1990), Flax.

(b) The French-based thinkers, introduced into American academia via the literature departments and consequently taken up mostly by scholars in the humanities and literary studies. By comparison, the works of the philosopher Irigaray (1974, 1977,

1984) have been translated into English as late as 1985. One of the immediate consequences of this effect of cultural export is that theories of sexual difference became synonymous with literature.[15] As a consequence, in the United States a hiatus was created between the humanities and philosophy and the social sciences.[16]

(c) The Italian group; here the key-figure is Irigaray. Whereas she was slow in coming into the English-speaking world (where Cixous swept in on the back of the Derrida fad), Irigaray found a fertile and receptive audience in Italy. Through the traditional links between the women's movement and the organized left-wing politics, Italian adaptations of Irigaray, especially by Muraro[17] and Cavarero (1990), produced a highly politicized version of sexual difference in terms of a social and symbolic alliance of women.[18]

(d) The lesbian radicalism of Wittig (1973, 1989) and Butler (1991).

(e) The ethnic and colonial thinkers.[19] Although in North American feminism the race issue had been present from the start, it took a long time for ethnicity and race to be recognized as a central variable in the definition of feminist subjectivity: the whiteness of feminist theory becomes the central target, overruling all other differences, including the previously polemical gap between "gender" and "sexual difference" theories. Accordingly, Spelman (1989) takes Beauvoir to task because of her colour-blindness and lack of sensitivity to the issue of ethnicity. The pioneer work of A. Lorde (1984), of black women writers such as A. Walker and T. Morrison and of many other black

---

15 See, for instance, Miller (ed.) 1986; Jardine 1985; Schor in Jardine and Smith (eds.) 1987; Spivak 1987; and Stanton's critique of Cixous, Irigaray and Kristeva in Miller (ed.) 1986.

16 This was evidenced by the special issue of the journal *Hypatia* On French feminist theory (3/1989).

17 Muraro 1991. See also the Milan collective volume on *Sexual Difference* (1990).

18 For a good presentation of Italian feminism in English, see Bono and Kemp (eds.) 1991.

19 An important landmark in this tradition is Hull, Bell, Scott and Smith (eds.) 1982.

theorists,[20] was followed by more systematic methodological critiques of the whiteness and the ethno-centrism of feminist theories of gender and sexual difference — such as those of G. Spivak (1990), C. Mohanty (1987, 1988), B. Smith,[21] Trinh Minh-Ha (1989). This enormous output by women of colour affected radically the thinking of feminist theorists such as de Lauretis, but also Haraway (1990) and the latest S. Harding.[22]

The new theorists emerging in the 1990's are consequently working along the lines of a multiplicity of variables of definition of female subjectivity: race, class, age, sexual preference and life-styles count as major axes of identity. They therefore innovate on the classical notion of materialism, in that they are bent on redefining female subjectivity in terms of a network of simultaneous power-formations. I will argue next that a new trend seems to be emerging that emphasizes the situated, specific, embodied nature of the feminist subject, while rejecting biological or psychic essentialism. This is a new kind of female embodied materialism.

Central to this new feminist materialism that rests upon the poststructuralists' redefinition of the text and of the relation of knowledge to power is the work of T. de Lauretis (1986, 1987). Starting from the co-extensivity of the text with material power-formations, de Lauretis invites us to reconsider the process of constitution of subjectivity as part of this network of power and knowledge. De Lauretis' insight can be summed up as follows. What if the patriarchal mode of representation, which can be named the "gender system", produced the very categories that it purports to deconstruct? Taking gender as a process, de Lauretis emphasizes a point that Foucault had already brought to our attention, namely that the process of power and knowledge also produces the subject as a term in that particular process. Basing his analysis of subjectivity on the co-extensivity of power and the process of becoming-subject, de Lauretis borrows the foucauldian

---

20 See, for instance, Moraga and Anzaldua 1981, 1983.

21 B. Smith 1983; and in Showalter (ed.) 1985.

22 Harding 1991.

notion of "technology of the self" to express the material foundations of this vision of the subject and, more importantly, of the ways in which gender functions.[23]

In other words, what lies at the heart of de Lauretis' redefinition of gender as the technology of the self is the notion of the politics of subjectivity, in the two-fold sense of both the constitution of identities and the acquisition of subjectivity meant as forms of empowerment, or entitlements to certain practices. The French term "assujettissement" renders both levels of this process of subjectification: it is both a material and a semiotic process that defines the subject through a number of regulative variables: sex, race, age etc. The acquisition of subjectivity is therefore a process of material (institutional) and discursive (symbolic) practices, the aim of which is both positive — because they allow for forms of empowerment; and regulative — because the forms of empowerment are the site of limitations and disciplining.

The key notion here is that of gender as a *regulatory fiction,* that is to say a normative activity which constructs certain categories, such as masculine, feminine, heterosexual and lesbian, as part of its very process. This idea of "gender" as a regulatory fiction must be read in the framework of the notion of "identity politics", that is to say the critique of the ethno-centric and univocal meaning of "gender". Foremost among this criticism of gender is the work of the "post-colonial" and the black feminist theorists quoted above.

To sum up this change of perspective in feminist theory, I would say that at the beginning of the 1990's a paradox has emerged. The paradox of feminist theory at the end of this century is that it is based on the very notions of "gender" and "sexual difference", which it is historically bound to criticize. Feminist thought rests on a concept that calls for deconstruction and de-essentialization in all of its aspects. More specifically, I think that over the last ten years the central question in feminist theory has become: how to

---

23 For a definition of the "technology of the self" see Foucault 1984, vol. II and III; and also my reading of this scheme of subjectivity (1991).

re-assemble a vision of female subjectivity after the certainties of gender-dualism have collapsed, privileging notions of the self as process (Scott), complexity (Braidotti), inter-relatedness (Haraway), post-colonial simultaneities of oppression (Spivak, Mohanty et alia) and the multi-layered technology of the self? In other words, the social and symbolic fate of *sexual polarisations* is at stake here.

The existential difficulties experienced by this new situation of the subject can also be documented socially: our era is marked by the phenomenon of "gender-bending", that is to say the gradual effacement of differences between the sexes in fashion, body appearances, hair-style and general behaviour. This phenomenon, which E. Showalter calls "sexual anarchy", expresses the deeper dislocations that have taken place in our culture about the structure and the regulatory function of gendered identities.

On a more theoretical plane, what I see as the central issue here is that of *identity as a site of differences*; feminist analyses of the gender system show that the subject occupies a variety of possible positions at different times, across a multiplicity of variables such as sex, race, class, age, life-styles etc. The challenge for feminist theory today is: how to invent new images of thought which can help us think about change and changing constructions of the self. Not the staticity of formulated truths or ready available counter-identities, but the living process of transformation of self and other.

4. *Beyond Gender?*

I will now proceed to outline two examples of recent thinking on gender from within the radically new perspective I have been defending here. I have chosen these particular examples as emblematic of the evolution in feminist theory that strikes me as a positive and illuminating change.

The first example I have chosen is J. Butler's re-reading of M. Wittig (1991), in which she starts by noting that feminist theory has inherited the dualistic opposition sex/gender which is the pillar of phallo-logocentric thought and which feminism is committed to deconstructing. Furthermore, she argues, theories of gender assume and imply a subject — woman who is represented as having certain attributes that feminist theory seeks to analyze and to correct. "Gender" is a regulatory notion because it presupposes and therefore it re-asserts a definition of "woman" that is highly prescriptive. In other words, to paraphrase T. de Lauretis, there is a culturally dominant definition of Woman that is a normative figuration of female subjectivity and it conceals the variety of differences that characterize women. The distinction between Woman and women marks both an epistemological and a political shift away from male-dominated definitions of women, towards the empowerment of alternative views of female subjectivity.

Butler's original contribution consists of emphasizing that gender sustains the normative "master-narrative" of heterosexuality; in other words, the cultural investment in certain ideas of Woman as opposed to the variety of ways of being by women keeps up the inner coherence of what A. Rich had rightly defined as "compulsory heterosexuality" and, by the same token, conceals the possibility of many other gendered identities. Gender is a patriarchal plot that upholds the heterosexual norm. In Butler's interpretation, "gender" ceases to be a concept and becomes an activity: it is the activity that constructs categories such as "sex", "women", "men" etc. for the explicitly political purpose of reproducing the heterosexual "institution" (in Foucault's sense of the term). Gender is the process by which women are marked off as the second sex, men are conflated with the universal and both sexes are subjugated to a normative view of sexuality.

Next, Butler takes up Wittig's case against "woman", which she sees as a fictional idea created by the patriarchal imaginary; she proposes that we dismiss this signifier as epistemologically and politically inadequate and that we replace it with the notion of "lesbian". The lesbian is no longer a woman because she has subtracted herself from identities based on the phallus: she is subversive because she refuses to uphold the heterosexual matrix and thereby she problematizes the whole scheme of sexuality. Radicalizing Wittig, Butler encourages us to approach gender as a *performative notion*, that is to say as the activity of *acting as* men or women. She translates this into the idea of a new subversive politics, *the politics of the masquerade*, which stresses the production of alternative gendered identities in a deliberate blurring of sexual boundaries and sexed identities. In a sort of political defense of the transvestite posture, Butler argues for the position of "beyond gender" as the subversive political gesture.

The second example I would like to draw attention to is Donna Haraway's work on the feminist subject as cyborg. Haraway is especially important for feminist theory because of her redefinition of materialism: she addresses issues related to science and technology in a non-nostalgic creative manner. Situating herself in what I would call the "post-humanist" vision of subjectivity, Haraway addresses the question of modernity in all of its force. The question is: how to be in a position of constructive opposition, while maintaining an adequate level of understanding of the complex structures of contemporary culture ? The post-humanist universe is defined by the dominance of the techno-scientific discourse, the omnipresence of mass-communication and the threat of ever-powerful death and life technologies. Haraway's question is: how can feminists propose a reasoned critique of scientific reason, while viewing science not as the main enemy but as a source of inspiration and even admiration? Haraway recommends that feminists develop new forms of literacy in order to decode today's world.

"Figurations" is the term Hawaray employs to stress the importance of finding adequate forms of representation for the new theoretical insights gained through feminism. A figuration is both a figure of speech and a new paradigm, that is to say a new theoretical practice suited to the feminist epistemological and political experience. Related to this point is the notion that critical intelligence is a form of empathy and that one cannot know properly, or even begin to understand, that towards which one has no affinity. In order to criticize, one must first understand and understanding requires affinity.

Haraway proposes the image of the "cyborg" as a suitable representation of the feminist knowing subject. The cyborg is a creature in a non-dualistic and therefore a post-gender world, outside the symbolic system centered on the phallus, which is dominated by the oedipal scheme of differentiation with the corollary of the pre-oedipal symbiosis. The cyborg is the post-nuclear and the post-metaphysical representation of a subject that is no longer universalistic. It does not claim to represent the generic human viewpoint, but rather recognizes and even embodies the specificity of spatio-temporal locations. The recognition of specificity, however, is no mere relativism: being situated somewhere is rather the pre-requisite for avoiding normative, regulative, hegemonic and exclusionary forms of thought.

To lay emphasis on the fact that "situatedness" is other than relativism, Haraway defines the cyborg or body-machine as a connection-making entity, a figure of inter-relationality, receptivity and communication. The cyborg as hybrid and as a figure of mixity between the human and the technological answers the difficult questions: How do we figure a collective non-generic feminist humanity? How do we reconcile the radical historical specificity of women with the insistance on constructing new figurations of humanity as a whole? Haraway emphasizes the situated embodied specificity, as opposed to disembodied abstract thinking. This leads her to postulating the idea of "situated knowledges", that is to say a multi-faceted foundational theory for an anti-relativistic acceptance of differences, in a historically-located semiotic and material subjectivity that seeks for connections and articulations in a non-gender-centered and non-ethnocentric perspective.

The cyborg is a figuration of the post-gender world in that it is defined by a multiplicity of variables that does not privilege sex over any other. Translated methodologically, this results in an approach of genealogical accounting for the constitution of embodied subjectivities, i.e.: to account for the making of certain kinds of subjectivities, situated in a specific social context. This form of genealogical accountability is Haraway's answer to the question of how to ground a new epistemology and a situated ethics.

These two attempts to theorize a post-gendered subjectivity can also be seen as attempts to speak of differences as positivities, not as subordinated forms of being. This may appear utopian in that it is so far removed from the ways in which subjects are constructed right now; but feminists like Irigaray also remind us that utopia means nowhere: the no-whereness of female subjectivity in the patriarchal system. Feminism is going to ground and legitimate the female subject; in other words, what emerges from these new developments in feminist theory is the need to recode or rename the female feminist subject not as yet another sovereign, hierarchical and exclusionary subject, but rather as a multiple, open-ended, inter-connected entity. To think constructively about change and changing conditions in feminist thought today, the emphasis necessarily falls on a vision of the thinking, knowing subject as not-one but rather as being split over and over again in a rainbow of yet uncoded and ever so beautiful possibilities.

Postscript

In the discussion Fokkelien van Dijk remarked that it had become clear to her that, in order to avoid any suggestion of neutrality with regard to the gender concept, the title "Gender and Theology" indeed appears to require a sequel. The focus of the Research Program being on women, and on the mechanisms of marginalization of women, this should be shown in the title. I added to that that I consider the challenge posed by feminist theologians to the universalistic tendency of much theological language as extremely important. The gender concept used as a verb, as it is done in Brenner's and van Dijk's study *On Gendering Texts*, can be very helpful in this respect. The concept, in this way, loses its static nature and shows its process-like character. Gendering biblical texts, for instance, turns from a quest for the author's gender into a search for the *voice* speaking in a text. Whether this voice will be recognized as an F (female/feminine) voice or an M (male/masculine) voice depends to a large extent on the reader's membership to a gender or, rather, on the gender role the reader takes upon herself or himself. Many biblical texts then appear to be potentially dual-gendered. "F readers will listen to F voices emanating from those texts; M readers will hear themselves echoed in them. This is to say that, in many cases, two parallel readings are possible" (Brenner and van Dijk-Hemmes 1993: 9). In other words, the so called dual-gendered texts tell a different story, depending on whether they are read as M texts or F texts.

This interesting and, at the same time, playful adaptation of the concept of gender-as-a-verb is not only intellectually satisfying but also politically relevant.

References

Benhabib, Seyla and Cornell, Drucilla, *Feminism as Critique,* Minneapolis, Minnesota University Press, 1987.

Benjamin, Jessica, *The Bonds of Love,* New York, Routledge, 1990.

Bono, Paola and Kemp, Sandra (eds.), *Italian Feminist Thought,* Oxford, Blackwell, 1991.

Braidotti, Rosi, "The Politics of Ontological Difference", in T. Brennan (ed.), *Between Feminism and Psychoanalysis,* London, Routledge, 1989.

——, *Patterns of Dissonance,* Cambridge, Polity Press/ New York, Routledge, 1991.

——, "Essentialism", in E. Wright (ed.), *Dictionary of Feminism and Psychoanalysis,* London, Routledge, forthcoming.

Butler, J., *Gender Trouble,* New York, Routledge, 1991.

Cavarero, Adriana, *Nonostante Platone,* Roma, Editori Riuniti, 1990.

Cixous, H., "Le rire de la Méduse", *L'Arc* 61 (1974).

——, *La Jeune née,* Paris, U.G.E, 1975.

——, *Entre l'écriture,* Paris, des femmes, 1986.

——, *Le livre de Promethea,* Paris, Gallimard, 1987.

Duchen, Claire, *Feminism in France,* London, Routledge & Kegan Paul, 1986.

Eisenstein, H., *Contemporary Feminist Thought,* Sydney, Allen & Unwin, 1984.

Foucault, M., *L'Ordre du discours,* Paris, Gallimard, 1977.

——, *Histoire de la sexualité,* Paris, Gallimard, 1984, vol. II and III.

Fuss, D., *Essentially Thinking,* London, Routledge, 1990.

Gallop, Jane, *Around 1981,* New York, Routledge, 1991.

Gilligan, Carol, *In a Different Voice,* Cambridge, Harvard University Press, 1982.

Haraway, Donna, "Gender for a Marxist Dictionary: The Sexual Politics of a Word", *Simians, Cyborgs and Women,* London, Free Association Books, 1990.

Harding, S., *The Science Question in Feminism,* Ithaca, Cornell University Press, 1986.

——, *Feminism and Methodology,* London, Open University Press, 1987.

——, *Whose Science? Whose Knowledge?, Thinking from Women's Lives*, Milton Keynes, OpenUniversity Press, 1991.

Hull, G. T., Bell Scott, P., Smith, B. (eds.), *But Some of Us Are Brave*, New York, Feminist Press, 1982.

Irigaray, L., *Spéculum*, Paris, Minuit, 1974.

——, *Ce sexe qui n'en est pas un*, Paris, Minuit, 1977.

——, *L'Éthique de la différence sexuelle*, Paris, Minuit, 1984.

Jardine, Alice, *Gynesis*, Ithaca, Cornell University Press, 1985.

Jouve-Ward, Nicole, *White Woman Speaks with Forked Tongue*, London, Routledge, 1991.

Lauretis, T. de, *Alice Doesn't*, Bloomington, Indiana University Press, 1984.

——, (ed.), *Feminist Studies/Critical Studies*, Bloomington, Indiana University Press, 1986.

——, *Technologies of Gender*, Bloomington, Indiana University Press, 1987.

——, "The Essence of the Triangle, or Taking the Risk of Essentialism Seriously", *Differences* 1/2 (1988), 3-37.

——, "Eccentric Subjects: Feminist Theory and Historical Consciousness", *Feminist Studies* 16/1 (1990), 115-150.

Lorde, A., *Sister Outside*, Trumansberg, N.Y., Crossing, 1984.

The Milan Women's Bookshop, *Sexual Difference: A Theory of Political Practice*, Bloomington, Indiana University Press, 1990.

Miller, Nancy, (ed.), *The Poetics of Gender*, New York, Columbia University Press, 1986.

——, "Subject to Change", in T. de Lauretis (ed.), *Feminist Studies/ Critical Studies*, Bloomington, Indiana University Press, 1986.

——, *Getting Personal*, New York, Routledge, 1991.

Minh-ha, Trinh, *Woman, Native, Other*, Bloomington, Indiana University Press, 1989.

Mohanty, C., "Feminist Encounters: Locating the Politics of Experience", *Copyright* 1 (1987).

——, "Under Western Eyes: Feminist Scholarship and Colonial Discourse", *Feminist Review* 30 (1988).

Moraga, C. and Anzaldua, G., *This Bridge Called My Back*, Watertown, Persephone, 1981.

——, *Loving in the War Years,* Boston, South End, 1983.

Muraro, Luisa, *L'Ordine simbolico della madre,* Roma, Editori Riuniti, 1991.

Rich, A., *Of Woman Born,* New York, Norton, 1976.

——, *On Lies, Secrets and Silence,* New York, Norton, 1979.

——, *Blood, Bread and Poetry,* London, The Women's Press, 1985.

Rubin, Gayle, "The Traffic in Women: Notes on the Political Economy of Sex", in R. Rapp (ed.), *Towards an Anthropology of Women,* New York, Monthly Review Press, 1975.

——, "Savoir et différence de sexes", *Cahiers du Grif* 45 (1990).

Schor, Naomi, "Dreaming Dissymmetry", in Alice Jardine and Paul Smith (eds.), *Men in Feminism,* New York, Methuen, 1987.

——, "This Essentialism That Is Not One", *Differences* 1/2 (1988).

Scott, Joan, "Deconstructing Equality versus Difference", *Feminist Studies* 14/1 (1988), 33-50.

——, "The Usefulness of Gender as a Category of Historical Analysis", *The Politics of History,* New York, Columbia University Press, 1990.

Smith, B., *Home Girls: A Black Feminist Anthology,* New York, Kitchen Table Press, 1983.

——, "Towards a Black Feminist Criticism", in E. Showalter (ed.), *The New Feminist Criticism,* New York, Pantheon, 1985.

Snitow, Ann, "Gender diary", in M. Hirsch and E. Fox-Keller (eds.), *Conflicts in Feminism,* New York, Routledge, 1991.

Spelman, Elizabeth, *Inessential Woman,* Boston, Beacon Press, 1989.

Spivak, G., *In Other Words,* New York and London, Methuen, 1987

——, *In Other Worlds,* New York, Routledge, 1990.

Stanton, Dona, "Difference on Trial: A Critique of the Maternal Metaphor in Cixous, Irigaray and Kristeva", in N. Miller (ed.), *The Poetics of Gender,* New York, Columbia University Press, 1986.

Whitford, Margaret, *Irigaray: Philosophy in the Feminine,* London, Routledge, 1991.

M. Wittig, *Le corps lesbien,* Paris, Minuit, 1973.

——, "The Straight Mind", *Feminist Issues* 1/1 (1989), 103-111.

The Birth of Aphrodite[1]

Anne-Marie Korte

I intend to speak to you about the birth of Aphrodite. The wish to talk about it came to me, I must admit, somewhat by accident. About a month ago I visited Cyprus, where I was on holiday. I discovered that Cyprus proudly presents itself as the island of Aphrodite, the island of the Goddess of Love. Indeed, very old traditions mention that Aphrodite was born on the shore of this island.[2] And in the poetry of Sappho, for example, Aphrodite is called 'the Cyprian'.[3] Today, traces of Aphrodite are identified at many spots on the island. When you visit Cyprus, you cannot miss that; they keep telling you about Aphrodite's special connection with Cyprus all the time, and everywhere. She really is the patron saint of Cyprus, or at least of its tourist industry.

When I was travelling around on this island, I could not help wondering: Why, of all places in the Mediterranean area, is Aphrodite's homeland here on this island? Why does tradition tell us that she, the Goddess of Love, the Greek Venus, emerged from the sea right here? To be honest, the landscape of the island is neither very exciting nor very lovely, or mysterious. Here there are no impressive caves as in Crete, no spectacular places in the mountains as in Delphi, no lovely, fertile hills as in Olympia. From a romantic point of view it is difficult to imagine Cyprus as a favourite spot for any Greek God. In fact, the island is named after its largest and very old industry: the mining of copper. For

---

1 I want to thank drs. Magda Misset-van de Weg, who helped me generously in preparing the English version of this article.

2 Gimbutas 1982: 149; Walker 1983: 44-45; Larrington 1992: 68-69.

3 Barnard 1958; cf. also Friedrich 1978: 104-128.

thousands of years copper has been dug here. Many invaders from different cultures came and left their marks because of this industry. There are still big mining factories on the island today. Some of them are very much in evidence on the slopes of the mountains, looking like great dark wounds.

So, a growing curiosity came over me when I was making my pilgrimage to the traces of Aphrodite, as prescribed by my guide-book. My most astonishing experience was a visit to the so called birthplace of Aphrodite. This place is located somewhere on the south-western shore of the island, on a rocky coast. There I found myself looking at a bare, ordinary piece of rock in the sea. Not quite the sight you would expect to mark the birthplace of the Goddess of Love. In a moment I will tell you what I did to satisfy my curiosity about Aphrodite being born in Cyprus. But first I must tell you why I recall the bafflement I experienced in front of Aphrodite's birthplace today.

Looking at the research programs of theological women's studies that have been written recently reminds me in some ways of my visit to Aphrodite's birthplace. Not only the theological department of the Rijks Universiteit Utrecht,[4] but also the Katholieke Theologische Universiteit in Utrecht[5] and other institutes have recently presented research programs in theological women's studies for the first time. Why is it that looking at them is a bit like seeing a bare rock in the sea while expecting or hoping to see the birth of Aphrodite?

The point is not that I think that these programs are not good or interesting. On the contrary, and I am very glad that these plans and programs are being made and presented now. The point is that these programs, even though I participated in writing them

---

[4] See the contribution of Fokkelien van Dijk-Hemmes in this book.

[5] In september 1992 a research program in women's studies was presented at the Katholieke Theologische Universiteit in Utrecht under the title "Tradition and modernity". The participants in this program are doing research in the fields of philosophy, religious studies, talmudica, systematic theology and the history of church and theology.

myself, present me with a certain problem. Why do these programs reflect so little of all the interesting and exciting questions that we are dealing with in theological women's studies at the moment? In order to answer this question, I will take a look at the history of theological women's studies here in the Netherlands.

Eight years ago I participated in an examination of the development of theological women's studies in the Netherlands. Together with Jonneke Bekkenkamp and Freda Dröes, we inquired how feminist theology had made its entrance in our universities. The picture we painted at that time, in 1985, was made ten years after the introduction of feminist theology into the universities.[6] At that time we could conclude that nowhere in the world had feminist theology obtained a foothold in the universities as fast and as firm as it did in the Netherlands. Not only had a strong network of feminist study and action groups been built in the universities but, at the same time, a complete institutional structure for theological women's studies had been created. That structure consisted of specially appointed lecturers, required courses, education programs, curriculum advisers, and so on. This model was initiated by Catholic and Reformed theological faculties and was soon adopted by the state universities (with the exception of the Rijks Universiteit Leiden.)

I am inclined to say now that a great part of this success must be attributed to the increasing number of female students entering the theological universities and departments in that same period. The participation of female students between 1975 and 1985 rose from about 5% to almost 50% of the student population.[7] And thanks to the presence of women's studies, many female students not only started but also finished their study in theology. Women's studies created 'a room of one's own' for women within the academic theological study program. Thus, the universities' investments in womens' studies proved their worth in terms of the graduation of many female students.

6 Bekkenkamp 1986.
7 Cf. Bekkenkamp 1986: 25.

At that time we also took stock of the research that was being done in the field of theological women's studies. I must say now that our reports, published in the book *Van zusters, meiden en vrouwen* in 1986,[8] sounded fairly optimistic. Looking at the research that was done by lecturers and students, we noticed the beginnings of several very promising research programs. Let me give you some examples. For the Theological University in Kampen we predicted the rise of a school of critical feminist reading of K. Barth and F. Schleiermacher. In Tilburg, we foresaw studies into different kinds of feminist spirituality. In Nijmegen, we expected the elaboration of feminist theology related to critical social theories. And as for Utrecht, both at the Rijks Universiteit and the Katholieke Theologische Universiteit, we were convinced that feminist research would undertake large projects in social ethics as well as in biblical studies.

Obviously, we expected that these research programs would develop as fast as the education programs had done. Moreover, a special chair for Feminism and Christianity was established in 1983 at the Catholic University in Nijmegen. Hence, in 1985 there was much hope that research in theological women's studies would soon be started in more structurally and institutionally organised ways within the universities. But it did not quite turn out that way. What has made the development of research programs in theological women's studies so difficult? Looking back, I see at least three complications.

First, I have to point to the scientific self-definition of women's studies. By this I mean the self-evident, extremely critical stance towards 'regular' science. This approach does not apply to theological women's studies alone. It is a position that theological women's studies has in common with women's studies in every other discipline. Because of its own radical aspirations, women's studies has thought of itself as "doing science in a totally different way."[9] The fact of women becoming subject and object of

---

8 Bekkenkamp 1986: 27-229.

9 Cf. Bowles 1983; Harding 1983; Fox Keller 1985; Benhabib 1987; Tuana

scientific theory has been conceived as a scientific revolution in itself, a paradigm shift, the creation of a new discourse. Such a critical stance requires a fundamental revision of almost all previous scientific suppositions.

As the feminist philosopher Sandra Harding points out, the problem is not that we do not know how to deal with women's issues or with feminism in science. The point is that, because we are already dealing with women's issues and feminism, science itself turns out to be the problem.[10] And not a small one. Taking this issue seriously, many methodological questions arise and, moreover, it seems that these questions need to be resolved first and immediately.

As a matter of fact it took a lot of time to create the framework, the ways of asking questions, the climate of discussion, all of which are needed when you try to alter science in such a fundamental way. What I mean to say is that we did not or, perhaps, could not know all the implications of the highly critical stance we took. And we certainly did not know how much time and energy it would require to develop them. Research approaches to methods and epistemology themselves had to be developed anew.

When I look back at the inventory of 1985 I see that we noticed at that time the methodological importance of the concepts of 'women's experience' and 'contextuality' in theological women's studies. In the evaluation that Jonneke, Freda and I wrote, we argued for more critical research on these issues.[11] The dissertations in theological women's studies that have been published recently show how very intricate these methodological issues are.[12]

Second, the development of research programs in theological women's studies has been complicated by internal troubles at the

---

1989.

[10] Harding 1986.

[11] Bekkenkamp 1986: 301-323.

[12] Meyer-Wilmes 1990; Dresen 1990; Maeckelberghe 1991; Korte 1992; van Dijk-Hemmes 1992; van Heyst 1992. See also the discussions on methods in theological women's studies as published in: Bekkenkamp 1989; Maeckelberghe 1989: 212-217; Papavoine 1990; Bekkenkamp 1991: 247-266.

universities. Since the second half of the eighties there seems to be a constant flow of academic reorganizations, all centered round the actual or possible withdrawal of money. Dazzling, rapid changes have taken place in the organization and financing of academic research. Just when you are beginning to understand how to present your research and how to fill in the forms for money applications, a new system with new rules has already been created. Of course, this is not a problem only women's studies has to deal with. But the fact that women are still hardly present in the higher academic positions makes the problem far more serious, and this is especially true in the case of theology and religious studies.[13]

Some of you will object that all of this is about to change, because there are now many more women working at the universities and because there is a policy of affirmative action in many places. I must say that I am not as confident as that. Rosi Braidotti has, as I remember, spoken about a tragic history of women being eternally too late. When women arrive at the top, the place itself has already lost its importance and power. Sometimes I am afraid that Braidotti is right. For example, can it be a coincidence that now that women are starting to take part in the national research organisations like STEGON, these organisations are about to be liquidated?

Third, there is one more factor which complicates the development of research programs in theological women's studies. I have to speak about the other side of the initial success of theological women's studies. The progress of women's studies in theological departments turned out to have a negative effect too. In the past few years, the universities invested structurally and materially in lecturers and education programs in theological women's studies.

---

[13] Beside the withdrawal of money designated for research there is also a withdrawal of money related to the decreasing number of students in the field of theology. Due to this last factor, i.e. the growing lack of new registrations for academic theological studies, theological departments and universities are more and more forced to cut down expenses, reduce staff, or even shut down.

But their investment in the organization of research was incidental only, or was not effective. I remember a significant example. In 1987 the Katholieke Theologische Universiteit of Utrecht intended to spend some extra money on theological women's studies. Several proposals were made. In the end the University Board chose to spend the money on supporting their own education program. The Katholieke Theologische Universiteit of Utrecht employed — on a temporary basis — an extra temporary female supervisor because of the urgent needs and demands. The alternative they rejected was the employment of someone who would initiate a proper research program in theological women's studies.

The 'Verkennningscommisie Godgeleerdheid', i.e. the governmental comittee that screened the theological universities and departments in 1989, drew attention to this problem too. That committee explicitly warned the universities to take their investments in theological women's studies seriously. It appears that the universities act trendily for the time being, but without developing serious plans for investments in the advancement of women's studies in the long run.[14]

Now, just before you start to think that all this sounds rather depressing, let me change perspectives and tell you about the other side of the coin. In spite of all the complications I have mentioned, there really is a lot going on in cooperation and programming of research in theological women's studies. Since 1986, there are several informal and internal organisations for contact and exchange and for the support of individual research projects. In 1986 we founded a national organization for mutual support during the process of writing theological dissertations, the Onderlinge Promotie Promotie Network. In 1986 we also started the European Society for Women in Theological Research and a special series, *Proeven van vrouwenstudies theologie*, to publish try-outs of dissertation research.

---

[14] Smits 1989: 92-93.

But cooperation and planning of this kind of research is growing also in a more formal and institutional way. Last year I participated in a small task group of the STEGON (i.e. the National Organisation for the Financing of Theological and Religious Studies, about to be liquidated, as already mentioned). We were asked to sketch the outline of an interuniversity research program in theological women's studies.[15] We decided to start with an inventory — and not because we did not know about the many good and very interesting individual research projects that are being worked on at the moment. We made this overview because we wanted to know more about the links between these projects and the institutional frameworks. So we made official and inofficial inquiries, and came across some very interesting things.

First, when we had gathered all the information, we discovered that a lot more research is seen, named and marked as "theological women's studies" than we had imagined. This is remarkable, and it might mean that we have to accept that this kind of research can be done and perhaps even must be done in many different ways. Giving special attention to the position of women is of course not the same as, for example, developing feminist hermeneutics. But in both approaches "gender" is utilized as a relevant and fruitful category in theological and religious studies.[16]

---

[15] This research program has been presented in december 1992 and is entitled "Embodiment – textuality – contextuality."

[16] On theoretical grounds, I agree with Rosi Braidotti that it is necessary to critique thoroughly the actual use and the implications of the concept of "gender" and to be aware of "counterproductive" use of this concept. (See her contribution to this book.) But, on political grounds, I will not make a plea not to use this concept any longer. Instead of judging or banning the concept of "gender" itself, it seems to me far more fruitful to stimulate a broad discussion – or even fights – on the basis of actual and different uses of the concept and the results thereof. The fact that "gender" is becoming more and more visible and accepted as a relevant scientific category is probably an indication that *the concept itself* has lost its exclusive original and univocal "feminist" vigour and sharpness. However, that in itself does not mean that the term cannot figure or play a role of any importance any more in the fight over women's issues. On the contrary, the battle about different uses of 'gender' facilitates the fight.

Second, we came across something we already knew, namely that most feminist-theological research is done individually and at one's own initiative, and is barely stimulated structurally by the theological departments. But, at the same time, there is in the field of theological women's studies more cooperation and more participation in research programs than we had thought. Many feminist theologians are already taking part in theological, philosophical, ethical and other research programs. Alternatively, they participate in the research centers for women's studies, like the Belle van Zuylen Institute in Amsterdam, the Anna Maria van Schuurman Center in Utrecht, or the Center for Women's Studies in Nijmegen.

Third and finally, our inquiries showed that some very important and promising kinds of research in theological women's studies are not related to any institutional frameworks as yet. For the continuation of these kinds of research we need to have our own research programs under the title of "Theological women's studies". It now becomes clear why the initiative of the theological department of the Rijks Universiteit Utrecht to start such a program is so important. Establishing women's studies research programs in theological and religious studies really means the creation of continuity as well as new possibilities. But it also means creating new challenges to deal with.[17] For instance, it demands the development of an interdisciplinary approach for women's studies, starting within our own disciplines of the theo-

[17] I would like to stress that it is important not to be too implicit about the theological moments in these research programs. On the one hand, as regards content, it is important to stress the visionary, utopian moment. And on the other hand, we need to be explicit for political reasons, to prevent fundamentalism and neo-orthodoxy from taking theology over. At the moment, attempts to revitalize theology seem to be coming strongly from the side of fundamentalist and neo-orthodox movements. But feminist theology is one of the most vital religious movements today also. It is a movement wherein religious belief, modernity and secularity do not simply clash, but actually meet in their own way. Therefore, as feminists and theologians we should not discard our ambivalences but, instead, work on them. We need to claim theology for our own purposes, our own projects and visions, at least because fundamentalism holds no promises for women.

logical departments. This approach has not been developed yet but we really cannot do without. In my opinion, this lack is part of the explanation why the research programs that are being made and presented now look somewhat like stones that mark the birthplace of Aphrodite.

I conclude — as promised — by telling you what I did about my questions on Aphrodite's being born on Cyprus.

Mary Daly has stated over and again that it is of great importance to take myths seriously. From a feminist point of view we should never underestimate the power of myths. To Mary Daly, all myths and all religious imagination worldwide reflect somehow or other the repression of the power and value of women.[18] The feminist theologians Carol Christ and Catherine Keller have shown that it is also possible to look at old myths a bit more lightheartedly. Using archaeological, historical and psychological insights in a creative way, they suggest that thinking about myths can be a playful way of commenting critically upon facts and opinions that are taken for granted.[19] I would add that this is possible because, in most cases, myths themselves deal with things and situations that are not taken for granted. A first clue in the case of Aphrodite and Cyprus came to me on reading a book by the cultural anthropologist and classicist Paul Friedrich, which was published in 1978.[20] In this book Friedrich writes on the meaning of Aphrodite in great detail. He starts with an interesting question, namely: Aphrodite is very important and prominent in Greek myths and in local traditions — why then is she silenced and avoided in academic research so often? This must be caused by the fact that there is something very uncomfortable about her, writes Friedrich. She is the Goddess of sexual love and of sensuality and, at the same time, of fertility and life-giving. For Friedrich, this makes her different from all other female Gods in Greek myths. In his opinion, Aphrodite is difficult to deal with

18 Mary Daly 1973, 1978, 1984.
19 Christ 1987; Keller 1986.
20 Friedrich 1978.

because of this combination of sexuality and fertility. She is sexually active/attractive and, simultaneously, motherly. But, according to Friedrich, that need not be a problem. He attempts to explain at length that, for women, making love and giving birth is very much alike physically.[21]

Of course, what we see at work here is a well known and classical gentlemen's obsession on how to deal with the fact that women can be mothers, and sexually active/attractive as well. Instead of studying this as his own or many men's problem, Friedrich tries to find a solution in studying women's bodily functions. But the direction Friedrich points to is interesting. I mean the idea that Aphrodite is really an uncomfortable Goddess to deal with, and that it is the combination of explicit sexuality and the power of fertility that brings about this uncomfortable feeling. It is no coincidence that Aphrodite is so often presented as a young, attractive woman, a playmate, a romantic and innocent figure, like for example in the Cyprian tourist industry. This covers up her ambivalence and her frightening aspects.

More recent feminist research on Aphrodite confirms this tendency to tame Aphrodite. In old texts and local traditions, Aphrodite has many clear traces of her original affiliation with the great Mother Goddess in whom sexuality, fertility and the power over life and death were not split yet.[22] We must keep this in mind when we want to know why tradition tells us that Aphrodite was born on Cyprus. A second clue came to me by reading a book by the feminist philosopher Carolyn Merchant. Her book, *The Death of Nature* (1980), presents an inquiry into the changing images of and attitudes towards nature in European history.[23] The thesis of her book is that an enormous shift took place in the treatment and the meaning of "nature" at the end of the Middle Ages and the beginning of the modern era. For Carolyn Merchant, this is a shift from nature seen as a living organism to nature seen and treated as a "machine". This shift is due to the

---

21 Friedrich 1978: 181-191.
22 Christ 1987: 105-115, 183-205; Smith, 1992: 65-101; Walker 1983: 44-45.
23 Merchant 1980.

growing possiblities to "explore" and "exploit" natural resources. It is the technological and scientific revolution of the modern era that has made this shift possible. This shift meant that the image of the earth as a living organism and a nurturing mother lost its meaning, its moral power and its spell. Carolyn Merchant tries to convince us that this is a serious loss. It means the disappearance of the idea that the natural environment draws its own lines, and deserves to be respected and honoured.

To illustrate this loss, Carolyn Merchant points to changing practices and attitudes towards mining.[24] Before the technological revolution that has made the commercial exploitation of minerals possible, mining was seen as entering into the veins or womb of mother earth, into a living female body. That is why ancient traditions speak of mining as a highly respected, almost holy profession. No entrance into the earth could be made without all kinds of rituals and preparations like praying, sexual abstinence and so on. But, far more important for Carolyn Merchant is the restricting ethics which come along with the idea of mining as entering the body of mother earth. She argues that the idea of the earth as a living organism and a nurturing mother has "morally restrictive" effects. In Greek and Roman texts, she states, we can find plenty of warnings against the mining of metals in the depths of the earth, out of concern for not violating mother earth. In the *Natural History* of Pliny, for example, we read warnings against exhausting the earth by penetrating her. No wonder, says Pliny, that the earth sometimes strikes back with earthquakes![25]

So, for Carolyn Merchant, what we have lost together with the image of nature as a nurturing mother is an "ethics of restriction" that is much needed at this moment. Well, if I turn to the case of Cyprus, I must challenge this vision. I find it too romantic and too normative. I have to ask the question: Has there ever been, in European history, such an ethics of restriction with regard to the natural environment, an ethics of restriction related to reverence for "mother earth"? In the second millennium B.C.E. Cyprus, the

---

[24] Merchant 1980: 20-41.
[25] Merchant 1980: 30-31.

island of Aphrodite, already had a very intensive and commercially oriented mining industry. Recent archaeological research has shown that, in the period of the two millennia before Christ, all the forests of Cyprus must have been burned down deliberately dozens of times. This huge amount of wood was needed to burn the ovens for the production of copper.[26] The mining industry must have also caused much pollution of water. So, the prosperity of the Cyprian inhabitants depended on endangering the natural environment on a very large scale for a very long time. Even the presence of Aphrodite, the Goddess directly related to mother earth, could not stop them.

This has made me think again about the relation between Cyprus and Aphrodite. Religious myths and images cannot be reduced to their esthetic, psychological or moral effects only. They are also tales of empowerment, hope and trust. Therefore, the question is not why Aphrodite belongs to Cyprus but, rather, why the Cypriots have defined themselves — and continue to define themselves — as belonging to Aphrodite. They did this, it seems to me, not in spite of the fact that they were putting their natural environment at risk, but because they were taking this risk. Because of the great risks they took, they needed the presence of Aphrodite, the Goddess of sexuality, fertility and the power over life and death.[27] The presence and the blessings of Aphrodite were needed in more ways than one. Aphrodite's presence was required, not only for the protection and prosperity of the earth but, and even more so, for the protection and prosperity of the people who are dependent on the earth.

So, finally, it is not surprising that Aphrodite's presence is still claimed by the Cypriots. And, perhaps, there is no place more appropriate for claiming her presence than in and for the tourist industry, on which the prosperity of Cyprus depends more and more today.

---

[26] This information is based on a temporary exhibition at the Cyprus Museum in Nicosia, which I visited on december 24th 1992.

[27] Confirmation for this vision is perhaps the fact that *copper* is the sacred metal that has been traditionally ascribed to Aphrodite. Cf. Walker 1983: 44.

References

Barnard, Mary [trans.], *Sappho: A New Translation,* Berkeley, University of California Press, 1958, no.37.

Bekkenkamp, Jonneke, et al. (eds.), *Proeven van vrouwenstudies theologie,* I, IIMO Research Publication; 25, Leiden/Utrecht, IIMO/IWFT, 1989.

Bekkenkamp, Jonneke, et al. (eds.), *Proeven van vrouwenstudies theologie,* II, IIMO Research Publication; 32, Leiden/Utrecht, IIMO/IWFT, 1991.

Bekkenkamp, Jonneke, Dröes, Freda, Korte, Anne-Marie (eds.), *Van zusters, meiden en vrouwen: Tien jaar feminisme en theologie op fakulteiten en hogescholen in Nederland,* IIMO Research Pamphlet; 19, Leiden/Utrecht, IIMO/IWFT, 1986.

Benhabib, Seyla and Cornell, Drucilla (eds.), *Feminism as Critique: On the Politics of Gender,* Minneapolis, University of Minnesota Press, 1987.

Bowles, Gloria and Duelli Klein, Renate (eds.), *Theories of Women's Studies,* London and New York, Routledge, 1983.

Christ, Carol, P., *The Laughter Of Aphrodite: Reflections On A Journey To The Goddess,* San Francisco, Harper and Row, 1987.

Daly, *Beyond God the Father: Toward a Philosophy of Women's Liberation,* Boston, Beacon Press, 1973.

——, *Gyn/Ecology: The Metaethics of Radical Feminism,* Boston, Beacon Press, 1978.

——, *Pure Lust: Elemental Feminist Philosophy,* Boston, Beacon Press, 1984.

Dijk-Hemmes, Fokkelien van, *Sporen van vrouwenteksten in de Hebreeuwse bijbel,* Utrechtse Theologische Reeks; 16, Utrecht, Faculteit der Godgeleerdheid, Universiteit Utrecht, 1992.

Dresen, Grietje, *Onschuldfantasieën: Offerzin en heilsverlangen in feminisme en mystiek,* Nijmegen, Sun, 1990.

Fox Keller, Evelyn, *Reflections on Gender and Science,* New Haven/Londen, Yale University Press, 1985.

Friedrich, Paul, *The Meaning of Aphrodite,* Chicago and London, The University of Chicago Press, 1978.

Gimbutas, Marija, *The Goddesses and Gods of Old Europe 6500 – 3500 B.C.: Myths and Cult Images* [sec. edn.], Berkeley and Los Angeles, University of California Press, 1982.

Gunew, Sneja, *Feminist Knowledge: Critique and Construct,* Londen/New York, Routledge, 1990.

Harding, Sandra and Hintikka, Merill B. (eds.), *Discovering Reality: Feminist Perspectives on Epistemology, Metaphysics, Methodology, and Philosophy of Science,* Dordrecht/Boston/Londen, D.Reidel Publishing Company, 1983.

Harding, Sandra, *The Science Question in Feminism,* Milton Keynes, Open University Press, 1986.

Heyst, Annelies van, *Verlangen naar de val: Zelfverlies en autonomie in hermeneutiek en ethiek,* Kampen, Kok, 1992.

Korte, Anne-Marie, *Een passie voor transcendentie: Feminisme, theologie en moderniteit in het denken van Mary Daly,* Kampen, Kok, 1992.

Keller, Catherine, *From a Broken Web: Separation, Sexism and Self,* Boston, Beacon Press, 1986.

Larrington, Carolyne (ed.), *The Feminist Companion to Mythology,* London, Pandora Press, 1992.

Maeckelberghe, Els, "Proeven van feministische theologie," *Lover: Literatuuroverzicht voor de vrouwenbeweging* 16 (1989).

——, *Desperately Seeking Mary: A Feminist Appropriation of a Traditional Religious Symbol,* Kampen, Kok Pharos, 1991.

Merchant, Carolyn, *The Death of Nature: Women, Ecology and the Scientific Revolution,* New York, Harper and Row, 1980.

Meyer-Wilmes, Hedwig, *Rebellion auf der Grenze: Ortsbestimmung feministischer Theologie,* Freiburg/Bazel/Wenen, Herder, 1990.

Papavoine, Marian, "Feministisch-theologisch onderzoek in Nederland," in: Bekkenkamp, Jonneke, et al. (eds.), *Proeven van vrouwenstudies theologie,* II, 247-266.

Papavoine, Marian and Kosterman, Anja (eds.), *Tussen beweging en wetenschap: Teksten IWFT-conferentie 11 en 12 mei 1990,* IWFT-Teksten; 1, Utrecht, IWFT, 1990.

Smith, Barbara, "Greece," in: Larrington, Caroline (ed.), *The Feminist Companion to Mythology,* London, Pandora Press, 1992.

Smits, A.H., et al., *Rapport van de Verkenningscommissie Godgeleerdheid*, I, Den Haag: Ministerie van Onderwijs en Wetenschappen, maart 1989, 92-93.

Tuana, Nancy, *Feminism and Science,* Bloomington and Indianapolis, Indiana University Press, 1989.

Walker, Barbara G, *The Woman's Encyclopedia of Myths and Secrets*, San Francisco, Harper and Row, 1983.

On Prophetic Propaganda and the Politics of "Love"

Athalya Brenner

1. *On "Prophetic" Authority and the "Love" Metaphor*

Let us agree that the Hebrew Bible or, if you wish, the "Old Testament", is a political document. It contains ideologies of specific interest groups. It is used for achieving political ends. It exercises fundamental influence on believers, has cultural significance for non-believers. It is therefore as important to resist its unpleasant features as to celebrate its values and beauty. This afternoon we shall therefore look at the flip side, at some sexist prophetic propaganda. If it were published elsewhere and today, such propaganda would have surely caused a public uproar; or, at the very least, it would be loudly challenged by feminists. We shall look at the development and utilization of one metaphor in Jeremiah: the metaphor of the divine, loving husband and his adulterous wife.

In our cultural discourse, prophetic books tend to have a privileged status that is similar to that of the Torah and the Psalms. When we discuss so-called prophetic writings we assume, explicitly or implicitly, that a real person, a real "prophet", resides in them. We say that the prophet "hears", "says", "suffers". Perhaps we need to avoid such complicity with the text. Perhaps we should remember that history, and scholarly criticism, do not necessarily support the claims those privileged texts make for themselves.

Take Jeremiah. Was the man so named real (in the sense of "historical"), or is "he" an imaginary, fictive figure? Did "he" perceive "himself", did "his" audience perceive "him", to be a prophet — which the God-in-the-text certainly did (1:5), as did later compilers and editors and interpreters? Should contemporary readers regard the book attributed to "him", a book whose boundaries in various biblical traditions are fluid, as prophecy? Let us remember that the referents of the Hebrew נביא, נבואה ("prophet", "prophecy") and their derivatives are far from agreed upon. I therefore prefer to regard the texts attributed to the real or literary Jeremiah, and to other "prophets", as poetry rather than prophecy.[1] An obvious advantage of such an approach is that it facilitates the crossing of a barrier. Poetic authority is easier to undermine than so-called prophetic authority.

The Jeremian passages to be discussed are, primarily, chapter 2; 3:1-3; and 5:7-8. Like in Hosea and Ezekiel, Israel and Judah (or Samaria and Jerusalem) are metaphorized into a faithless wife and a *zônāh*. YHWH, the metaphoric male counterpart, is the faithful husband who is deeply affected by his wife's misbehaviour. The descriptions of the wife's escapades and deserved punishment are vivid and detailed. As van Dijk-Hemmes demonstrated in her essay on Hosea (1989), metaphorized language of this sort may pervert the language of love. And in her essay on Ezekiel (1993) she traces some pornographic properties which underlie political and religious concerns within the presentation of the love metaphor in Ezekiel 23. In the biblical text, Jeremiah is situated between Hosea and Ezekiel. Let us see how the adaptation of the love metaphor fares in this midway position.

2. *The Metaphor as Propaganda*

To guess author's intent is a risky business. However, one must indulge in it in order to comprehend the metaphor's function. It seems that the poet whom the text calls "Jeremiah" wishes to tighten the bonds between his God and his target audience. It is thus fair to deduce that the husband-wife metaphor is a propa-

---

[1] See the dialogue in writing by Overholt, Auld and Carroll in Issue 48 of *Journal for the Study of the Old Testament* (1990: 3-54).

ganda vehicle whose employment is motivated by the following assumptions:
— The metaphorization of human sexuality is attractive enough for securing an audience's attention and for sustaining interest.
— In order to be effective, the metaphor should be recognized by the target audience as applicable to stock life situations or, preferably, as universally valid.
— Female sexual behaviour is recognized by speaker and audience as potentially deviant even when unprovoked by a male partner. Therefore it is a fitting vehicle for the message intended.
— Audience's involvement in and emotional response to the metaphor are expected.
— The audience may thus be trapped into identification with the speaker, to the point of accepting his message.
— The metaphor will produce guilt and shame in the audience through a rejection of the metaphorized female. The new consciousness will put an end to the illicit (from the speaker's perspective) religious and political alliances in Judah and Jerusalem.

3. *Sexual Imagery, or Pornography?*

In daily discourse many of us use love- and sex talk for communicating religious experience and vice versa — god-talk for sexual experience. This language practice is so common as to render the husband/wife metaphor unproblematic for both female and male readers. Furthermore, even when we agree that the metaphor's presentation in Hosea and Ezekiel contains pornographic elements, this does not absolve us from examining it afresh in the relevant Jeremian texts.

Is the husband/wife metaphor in Jeremiah pornographic, or is it "just" sexual imagery? Five steps will be taken towards an answer:
(1) The construction of a working definition of the term "pornography";
(2) a rereading of the Jeremian (or Hosean, or Ezekielan) metaphor;

(3) an examination of other metaphors and figurations of woman in Jeremiah;
(4) a comparison with another, contemporary ancient text which deals with gender roles; and finally,
(5) a reading of a comparable literary intertext outside the Bible, so as to double-check the findings of the previous steps.

Dictionaries define pornography as the explicit description or exhibition of sexual activity in literature, films and so on. The description or exhibition are designed to stimulate erotic response rather than aesthetic pleasure. Such a definition, although widely used in popular discourse, is inadequate. It does not relate to the issue of fantasy of desire which pornography activates; we shall return to the fantasy component presently. Furthermore, such a definition does not refer to social factors, least of all gender-specific factors. In order to redress the balance, any working definition has to be supplemented by incorporating data from feminist criticism in psychology, sociology, literature, and the arts.

Fantasy in pornography, like in rape, is not simply a fantasy of sex and desire. Pornographic fantasy incorporates elements of power, domination, gender relations, and quite often violence. Within the fantasy, desire becomes a metaphor which reflects social "reality". That metaphor feeds on imagination and fuels individual and collective dreams. It is both refractive and recreative. Pornographic presentations have social significance. Thus a definition must qualify the roles assigned to females (and minors; and minorities of class, colour, ideology, or ethnic origin) in contradistinction to males in pornographic presentations. The definition should also relate to the degree and nature of each gender's response to the presentation. I have no quarrel with the truistic presentation of sexual desire as a primary human motive; but defining pornography "objectively" as a stimulant to Desire, without taking socio-psychological factors into account, is at best misleading.

So we turn back to Jeremiah. Let us now ask, How does the erotic metaphor work beyond securing the audience's attention? It certainly stimulates sexual fantasy. It does something else as well. The eager presentation of deviant female sexuality — and details are liberally supplied — can have one purpose only: to *shame the audience.* The more blatant the presentation, the more shocking and shameful its referent, namely the people's fickleness in forming alliances. The result of this strategy is a contrast between the metaphor and its designated purpose: pornography is expected to promote religious and political reform.

Persuasion through stigmatization, shaming as a means of bonding, and the manipulation of love are practised inside family structures and outside them — in relationships with subordinates (like children), superiors (like parents) and peers. The manipulation of stigmatization and shaming is a powerful tool for attaining social and political gain. The stigmatization of sexual behaviour and its abusive presentation is a trick employed by children, for instance, before they even know what the words used designate. It is commonly targetted on weak social groups, be their constituency female or male. However, because women are a much weaker social group than their countergender, their stigmatization by pornographic presentation is much more common than that of males (Janeway 1989). This holds true for the Bible as well as for other literary and visual representations, ancient and modern alike.

The Jeremian passages afford illuminating examples of this principle. Indeed, male sexuality is attacked too; however, the description of male adultery and animalistic desire in 5:7-8 is a single occurrence. All other passages which belong to the divine husband/adulterous wife metaphor are resolutely devoted to inducing shame by reference to female sexual behaviour. The practice is admitted by some commentators but, unfortunately, its gender significance is seldom acknowledged. For instance, Robert Carroll recognizes that we deal with pornography here. He writes in his OTL commentary on Jeremiah,

> Since Hosea, religious pornography has become a standard form of abusing opponents. Once the metaphors of marriage are transferred to describing the relationship between Yahweh and Israel, then all the

> abuse that might be heaped on a faithless wife will become part of the arsenal of religious denunciations. This transference will explain the degree of emotion generated in such statements (Carroll 1986: 134).

I suggest that Carroll's reading is gendered by his male bias. Although he does not define what he means by "religious pornography", Carroll claims to *understand* the metaphor — although, to be fair, he does not appear to approve of it. When he goes on to warn against viewing the relevant texts as misogynistic, like some feminists do, he deconstructs himself completely. Indeed, an automatic equation of pornographic female representations and misogyny should not be adopted without due consideration. However, Carroll and other male commentators ignore some important issues. For instance: Whose fantasies are enacted in the prophetic love metaphor? Whose ends do such fantasies serve? How do they do it? Upon reflection, things are not so simple. Contemporary pornographic literature by and large contains an implicit anti-female bias; if we agree on that, the same notion is applicable to the pornographic prophetic texts — hence the benefit of a comparative approach.

A female reading of the love metaphor would have a different agenda, an agenda whose origin is undeniably biased and gendered too. It would not focus on the male figurations within the story — the metaphoric husband, the messenger's voice, God. Instead, it would focus on female figurations within pornographic representations; and would append additional criteria to those of erotic stimulation and sexual fantasy.

Contemporary feminist theories define pornography by distinguishing four categories: its *features, functions, definition,* and *causes* (Setel 1985: 87ff.). Van Dijk-Hemmes has applied the first two categories to Ezekiel 23 (van Dijk-Hemmes 1993). Here I shall apply all four to the Jeremian passages, then to my modern intertext, the *Story of O.*

4. *The Features of Pornography*

Female sexuality is pornographically (re)presented as negative in relation to a positive or neutral male sexuality. Women are publicly humiliated. Like nature and the land, they are subjected to male possession and control. They exist in order to gratify male desire — as do also minors and minorities in modern pornographic presentations.

Let us examine Jeremiah 2:23-25 for these features. Jerusalem, the community, is addressed by the speaker as YHWH's legitimate spouse. The words "nation", "community", "city", "land" are grammatically female in Hebrew. However, this does not adequately account for the gendering of the metaphor, or for the abuse of the metaphorical female it contains. Thus is the community addressed:

> How can you say, "I'm not defiled, I haven't followed the Ba'als"? See your way in the valley, know what you've done. [You're] a young camel deviating from her path; [you're] a wild she-ass accustomed to the wilderness, sniffing the wind in her lust. Who can repel her desire? All who seek her needn't exhaust themselves, for they shall find her in season... And you said, "No! I love strangers and will follow them".

In the metaphor, female sexuality is objectified as irregular and deviant. It is animalistic, "natural", earthy. The metaphorized female creature is motivated by neither love nor by any other acceptable human-social convention. She/it is motivated by lust. In contradistinction, male sexuality is represented by God's behaviour which, by definition, is politically, socially and morally correct. Since the "woman" is explicitly qualified as the legal possession of her male/God (vv. 20-21), her sexual conduct violates his rights; she is therefore punishable by public exposure, a measure for having degraded herself publicly. The same description recurs in ch. 3: the "woman" is reported to reside in nature; her passion is wild and unquenchable; her behaviour is shameful.

The animalization of the metaphorized "woman" is perhaps the most striking feature of Jeremiah 2, especially because it does not stop at the animalization stage. It is an innovation, a new development, an original contribution to prophetic pornography. It cannot be found even in the most enthusiastic pornographic descriptions of Ezekiel 16 and 23. In Ezekiel town, community and nation(s) are naturalized by their metaphorization into land/earth on the one hand and into women on the other hand. As Setel and van Dijk-Hemmes show, the two metaphors (earth and woman) are interlinked by a shared reference: the extra-linguistic association of woman with nature and especially the earth. This is common in pornographic as well as other texts. The establishment of a two-way link between woman and land facilitates an evolvement of the metaphor into the next stage. The naturalization of woman by animalization constitutes a powerful new phase in the ongoing construction of the husband/wife metaphor. This animalization cannot be waived aside as immaterial or gender-neutral. Its intent, and the value judgement it displays, are indicated by the animal referents chosen: a wild she-ass, a young she-camel, neither of which famous for redeeming features. The metaphorization of humans into animals is often pejorative or carries a sting: much depends on the animal referent chosen. Furthermore, the metaphorized "wild she-ass" is both more and less than a merely natural animal: whoever heard about an animal who is constantly in heat, forever lustful? Such an animal would not qualify as natural. She/it is fabulous, mythic. Thus, the animalization of woman imparts that "she" posits "herself" outside the human/social order by being (a) wild and (b) always in heat, hence (c) a mythological rather than natural creature. Let us remember: this fantasy of womanliness must correspond to a similar fantasy of the target audience in order for the propaganda to be effective. Disgust and shame will not be produced unless the listeners recognize the validity of the description for female sexual behaviour in general. That is imperative if they are to dissociate themselves from similar behaviour outside the sexual sphere. The dehumanization of the metaphorical woman is the analogy chosen to reflect the condemned, inhuman conduct of the extra-metaphorical referent, the addressed community. An interim stage in getting the message across is to reach out of language by appealing to desire and emotion. A recognition that women are (like) animals will make the metaphor work. This recognition need not be conscious. It will be as effective, perhaps more so, if it stimulates desire unconsciously. The hoped-for renunciation seems like one of the reasons for using pornographic images in the love metaphor. Is it as paradoxical as it sounds?

Does this new development express fear of the female and misogyny? If we readers feel that the textual voice disapproves of women as wild and [un]natural animals; that the target audience is drawn into sharing this disapproval; that the pornographic fantasy feeds on the view that female sexuality is uncontrollable — then, yes, misogyny underscores this dehumanized, animalized depiction. This is *not* "just a metaphor".

5. *The Function of Pornography*

The *function* of pornography is to maintain male dominance through the denial or misnaming of female sexual experience. Objectification of the female is presented as universally acknowledged instead of being attributed to male predisposition against femaleness. Women are expected to identify with this perspective, through which they may indiscriminately be imaged as prostitutes, harlots and whores (Setel 1985: 87-8).

In Jeremiah the "woman", the community, Judah and Jerusalem and/or Israel, is never asked to defend "herself": "her" voice is not heard, for an adulteress deserves to be punished by divorce without further argument (3:1, 8). The message to the target audience is: if you endorse the universal truth of the metaphorized female's behaviour as it is presented; if you, males, want to preserve male social supremacy, as does the speaker; if you, females, accept the fantasy's view of your gender; if you, the community, want to forsake pornography in favour of love and loyalty; if you-all consider the allocation of sex roles within the metaphor valid and appropriate for the relationship between God and his community — then, well, a basic rejection of female nature informs your receptivity. You seem to support male dominance not only in the divine sphere, but also in the human domain: the metaphor's ideology cuts both ways.

The metaphorized woman is repeatedly called *zônāh*, here and in Hosea and Ezekiel. It is not clear what exactly she is accused of.

Prostitution (the sale of her sexuality)? Harlotry (uncontrollable sexuality)? Whoredom (being backed by a male patron)? The distinction between the three (English) terms is blurred in the biblical text. To complicate matters further, adultery is apparently *zĕnût* too, as is being a *qĕdēšāh* (the translation "cult prostitute" affords a splendid example of biased interpretation). The semantic confusion in the biblical text is perpetrated by its interpretations (Bird 1989a, 1989b). The biblical discourse and its metadiscourse share common premises. The indiscrimination which both discourses share amounts to a gross misnaming of female experience. Addressees and readers alike are expected to identify with and adopt God's and the poet's indignation at the supposedly stereotypic female sexual behaviour.

6. *Feminist Definitions of Pornography*

Feminist definitions of pornography vary. However, most of them relate the functions of pornography, as presented earlier: pornography promotes the objectification and debasement of female persons and femaleness. It encourages female abuse and restricts female sexual choice to a state of virtual servitude. Consequently, male power is highlighted and legitimated (Setel 1985: 88). Reading Jeremiah 3 in this light yields unsurprising results. The figuration of one errant wife in ch. 2 has now blossomed into two errant wives. The same process is in evidence in Ezekiel: the metaphorization of one community into one wife in ch. 16 evolves into a double presentation of two communities as such wives in ch. 23. One makes two, and two lead to a generalization by drawing on male stereotypes of the female. It now becomes more evident that God/the male has been treated horridly by the wives he supposedly possesses. They (and they are actually one "woman", in the metaphor as in life and history, for they typify "woman") have attempted to choose their partners. They have forgotten their proper place. They/She are therefore guilty of social, moral, and legal transgressions. The pornographic presentation asserts male domination through the control of female sexuality.

Tracing the mechanism of persuasion, we notice that it moves subtly from the particular to the general, then to the ideological. Because the argumentation is analogic, its fallacy is tricky to pinpoint. Powerful gender conventions are at stake, and they are bound up with religious concerns. The enlistment of pornography as propaganda tool validates the metaphorized relationship between God and his community. This validation is accomplished by appealing to a familiar male view: women are by nature promiscuous, hence in need of containment.

7. *The Causes of Pornography*

Feminists recognize that the ultimate *causes* of pornography are male insecurity and male need to affirm and reaffirm control in the face of change (Setel). Therefore, pornographic propaganda in Jeremiah (and Hosea, and Ezekiel) reflects not only the poet's political and religious concerns but also his — whoever "he" may have been — psychological and social concerns as a male. The love metaphor is true M (Male/Masculine) literature, not just androcentric but truly phallocentric. Let us note in passing the preoccupation with male genitalia in the pornographization of males in Ezekiel 23.20 and Jeremiah 5.8. The husband/wife metaphor is woman-suspicious: especially wife-suspicious, so much so that it is expected to be convincing when delivered by a "Jeremiah", a fictive bachelor. However, verbal sexual abuse, like sexual jokes, exposes fascination and desire more effectively than it masks them (Freud 1976: 1981).

8. *Non-Pornographic Representations of Woman in Jeremiah*

To be sure, there are some non-pornographic representations of woman in Jeremiah: let us have a quick glance at them. Jeremiah 31 has a cluster of metaphorized, type-cast women: mother (v. 15), virgin (vv. 4, 21) and daughter (v. 22). However, the chapter contains no newly configured wife metaphor, which would have redeemed the previous love metaphor somewhat. The subject matter of ch. 31 is the imminent reversal of fortune for God's suffering community. Does this signify a change in role for the metaphorized females? The archmother Rachel feelingly weeps for her sons: she is totally preoccupied with her male children's fate, as a mother should. A dead mother is an asexual, safe object for veneration. Moreover, the community has miraculously become a virgin. A virgin is a better spouse for a male than a tainted wife. Fresh hopes for better male control this time? In addition to marital male authority, paternal authority is invoked too. When a "daughter" figure appears toward the end of the chapter, she is presented as exasperating and too tricky for male comfort. There is no erotic imagery in this chapter, no pornography. Nevertheless, the female images conform to the pattern established earlier and complement it through the suggested reversal. They constitute an additional transference of male concern about legitimate, properly allocated gender roles to religious discourse (and see van Dijk-Hemmes 1989).

There is birth imagery in another Jeremian passage (20:7-20; see Magonet 1987). This imagery has no relevance or redeeming grace for our topic either. Ultimately, it appears that in Jeremian pornography and outside it, disconnected images of woman reveal analogous attitudes. The difference in presentation between the husband/wife metaphor on the one hand and the mother, virgin bride, and daughter metaphors on the other hand resides neither in the contents nor in the underlying ideology of each particular case. Differences are superficial. They are conditioned by the vehicle chosen for presentation (the elected metaphors) and the message of each particular discourse.

9. *An Ancient Intertext: Semonides*

Suspicion of women in general and wives in particular has been expressed in androcentric literature from early antiquity on. A pertinent example is the work by the ancient Greek poet Semonides, dubbed by its English translator, Lloyd-Jones, "The first satire on women in European literature" (1975, so the subtitle). This work can serve as a suitable intertext to Jeremiah on a few counts. It advances outspokenly male perspectives about women. Chronologically, it is attributed to the 7th century BCE (which is the time slot claimed for the fictive Jeremiah too). It divides women-wives into ten categories, all metaphorized in terms of nature phenomena, eight of which are animals. The female imaged as an ass, central to the Jeremian metaphor, is present here too: "when she comes to the act of love, she accepts any partner" (English version, p. 44). This particular correspondence as well as the overall similarity between the two texts is interesting. But so are the differences. Although both poetic texts are informed by male suspicions and male needs, the Greek work refers to female sexuality in a non-pornographic manner. No stimulation of fantasy is attempted beyond the sentence quoted. This example illustrates that misogyny and pornography need not be literary bedfellows, which is what they are in the prophetic husband/wife metaphor.

10. *A Modern Intertext: the Story of O*

Let us move to consider a modern piece of pornography, our so-called control text, the *Story of O.* It was ostensibly authored by a woman, Pauline Réage (we shall return to the issue of authorship later). This popular French novel has been translated into several languages, filmed, and acclaimed as a breakthrough in female erotic prose by some male critics. Yet, and more widely, it is considered a pornographic novel which efficiently stimulates desire and fantasy while — like the husband/wife metaphor — betraying conventionalized social mores. Unlike prophetic literature, the *Story of O* is non-canonical. However, it has undeniable literary merit, which facilitates the comparison to the Jeremiah text. A comparison between the two works may in fact begin here. Literary merit may camouflage what should otherwise seem conspicuous — in the present case, the conspicuous constituent is the pornographic figurations of woman. The literary impact of the Jeremian passages is beyond dispute. This, in addition to its canonical status and the ideology it shares with many readers, disguises the methods employed and the underlying worldview.

Indeed, it must be admitted that in the prophetic metaphor pornography features as a means to an end, whereas in the *Story of O* it looks like an end unto itself. Nevertheless, I find the similarities between the two texts unsettling. This difference is certainly significant. And yet, in a way, prophetic pornography is more disturbing than other kinds of pornography, for prophetic literature is usually approved off unproblematically as religious instruction. At any rate, both texts represent their own "reality" inasmuch as relate to sexual desire.

O is a young woman in love who remains anonymous throughout the novel. The story charts a journey she agrees to undertake, a journey which is initiated by her male lover. She is gradually transformed into a naked and abused sex object whose physical or symbolic death is imminent by choice. Finally she becomes a non-person, a uterus controlled by her masters and open to all, an Orifice — but lo and behold, by her own testimony she celebrates her situation. She is aware of becoming reeducated through the intense didactic efforts of her male mentors, who have practised upon her every mental and physical violation their fantasy could invent. Now naked, with a chain through her genitals, with her skin branded, she is displayed as a constructive lesson for all nubile females to emulate. But she is jubilant: she realizes that she has fulfilled her destiny, the punishment and her masters' stamp makes her belong. Initially accused of being promiscuous by nature (She is a female, is she not?), O has achieved chastity and understanding of her true female nature through sadomasochism. Now she is ready to be reborn as a male-controlled submissive female who is devoted to the ideal praxis of her gender — a conscious, self-determined bondage of love. In short, O and the narrator assure us, O has achieved "genuine" feminine selfhood.

When Jessica Benjamin discusses *O* (1980, 1988), she points out that in the pornographic fantasy of rational[ized] violence, love, control and submission are intermingled (Benjamin 1980: 41). She attributes the fantasy of erotic domination to the process of differentiation between object and subject. In our culture this process entails a tension whose origin harks back to early infancy. That tension is seldom resolved successfully; instead, it is often dissolved into a gender split. Inflexible gender roles are ascribed to females and males. No mutual recognition is achieved. False nourishment is then derived by males and females from their dialectical master-slave relationship (after Hegel).

Benjamin's critique of the psycho-social factors operative in *O* is applicable to the Jeremian love metaphor too. A short comparison of individual details from the two texts will highlight their affinities further.

In the *Story of O* a reciprocal fantasy of one gender's control and the other gender's submission is expressed by the metaphor of sadomasochism. A divided mythic image is produced. Sadism represents maleness, masochism the essence of femaleness and femininity (see also Caplan 1987). In Jeremiah, the similar fantasy — suggested also in Hosea and Ezekiel — reaches a climax. A [male] fantasy of [male] domination is acted out by equating divine authority with male power. The [male] fantasy of [female] submission becomes definitive. It is easily legitimized by a two-way application of the analogy: when God is imaged as a human male, human males can be viewed as divine. This is how metaphors work: there is interaction between sign and referent inside the metaphorical vehicle, and this has consequences. Metaphor creates its own "reality", its own frame of reference, not to mention hierarchy. Benjamin's analysis implies that the choice of sexual metaphor is deeply rooted in male infantile fantasy. I'd like to add, though, that without female desire and complicity this fantasy would not work for the female members of an audience. Neither would the implied social order — patriarchal, androcentric, phallocentric- — be upheld.

There has been some controversy in feminist circles about the question, Is it possible that a woman wrote *O*, thus subscribing to male fantasy? Yes, of course; one gender's fantasy cannot survive without the cooperation of the other. But whether that reciprocation derives from one and the same source for both remains questionable. Whose [im]pure lust is it anyway?

O complies with the sadomasochistic procedures inflicted upon her willingly; she sees herself as a consenting subject. In her view, as narrated, she acquires a subject/partner's position by choosing to internalize her masters' value system. The consequences are the loss of her personal and sexual freedom, and the emergence of a heightened sense of shame and guilt. This is precisely what Judah, Jerusalem, Israel, the target audience, are being persuaded into doing in the Jeremian text: they are asked to acknowledge their so-called sinful ways, admit their guilt, and internalize it. They are urged to feel shame, guilt, remorse as a prelude to repentance. A refusal will be punished.

O, then, is no ordinary victim: she is co-producer of her own fate. She is convinced by her masters' verbal logic that her reeducation is necessary, that it will make her socially and morally acceptable, that it will make her desirable for male partners. Her biblical counterparts are presented as responsible for their own "deviant" behaviour and the dismal fate that awaits them if they do not obey. The textual speakers as well as the literary styles and voices are different in each case. Verbal violence parading as rational wisdom obtains in both texts.

O is requested to submit to the superior wisdom of her male mentors. The same goes for the biblical addressees in the love metaphor. They are asked to give up their independent judgement in favour of divine judgement. *O* is found guilty of promiscuity, hence the treatment she undergoes for her own good. Her boundaries are violated. She is stripped naked. This is education, designed to promote her spirituality. The analogy to the biblical communities addressed as women is clear. The prophetic male voice announces that those same things will be done to them in God's name in order to remake them suitable companions for him. O views herself as a subject but she in fact becomes a dependent sex object, whereas her masters retain their independence and subjectivity. The woman Judah/Jerusalem, or Israel/Samariah, is depicted as dependent on "her" God whereas he remains her independent master. He cares, to be sure; he desires loyalty from his woman, his people. However, his subjectivity does not stem from their recognition. Like O's lovers, YHWH's domination consists of his declared omnipotence, together with a denial of his women's separateness.

By the end of her story O has undergone a complete transmutation: from human to animal, then to an unnatural animal (a hairless owl woman). She is then possessed by her lovers in a manner reminiscent of sacrifice. The total control of the female, and her acceptance of that control, hang upon the completion of this transmutational process. The analogy to the community's animalization in Jeremiah is obvious. The textual masters, God and his messenger, intend to subjugate this animal. They are fascinated and attracted, their attitude is ambiguous. But, naturally, they know better than an unnatural animal does. Finally, O sees her experience as a spiritual and religious journey. In the prophetic metaphor the opposite obtains. Religious alliance is metamorphosed into a kind of "love". The two perspectives are different enough. And yet, they look too much like the two sides of the same coin. And that makes me feel uncomfortable. Actually, acutely uncomfortable.

11. *Personal Conclusions*

I am a woman, white, Western, Jewish, an Israeli, middle class, heterosexual, divorced, a mother, with an academic education. I hope that, over the years, my efforts to become an F (Female/Feminine) reader have been successful. So how am I to respond to the *Story of O*? I have two alternatives. The one is to identify with O, for her fantasy is — at least to a certain extent — my fantasy too, acquired by the socialization process I've undergone. The other option is to rebel against the myth of female masochism and female sexual objectification. I can refuse the recommendation, nay, instruction to achieve female selfhood at the price of independence. I can say, This is carrying things too far, this subordination of F fantasy to M fantasy. I do not want to be negated in order to join the symbolic male order. I am no prude; I can tolerate, sometimes enjoy, pornographic representations up to a point. But I cannot ignore the gendering effect most pornographic presentations have for persons who belong to the same anatomical sex as I do.

How am I to respond to the prophetic propaganda which depicts Judah and Jerusalem and Israel as an objectified spouse, an animalized it-woman? This propaganda cleverly constructs a stereotype: everywoman, especially everywife, is a potential deviant and should therefore be tightly controlled. By males, of course. Wife-abuse and rape should be directly linked to the worldview which makes such prophetic propaganda acceptable. Religious-political propaganda can lead to wholesale rape of women: read the news about Bosnia. So, once more, I have two alternatives. The one is to identify with the male poet's viewpoint, which is presented as God's viewpoint. The other option is to resist the kind of "religious pornography" which is characteristic of the husband/wife metaphor. I can object to the socio-cultural role implied by the metaphor *and* its proponents, no matter whether consciously or otherwise, for persons gendered as "females".

Toward the end of her analysis, Jessica Benjamin writes: "...The same psychological issues run through both political and erotic forms of domination, for they both embody denial of the other subject" (1980: 66). Religious domination, be it morally just or otherwise, undoubtedly belongs to the category of political domination. And on that note, I come to my conclusion.

The religious propaganda of the prophetic love metaphor abuses female sexuality although, to be sure, it attacks male sexuality too. I do not know whether a historical person named Jeremiah (or Hosea, or Ezekiel) was responsible for the pornographic passages which bear that name in our canon. Hence, the metaphor should not be dismissed on the grounds that "he", the prophet, was unfortunately motivated by "his" own personal circumstances. Instead, I would like to point out that whoever composed these passages perceived men, God, women, and gender relations in a certain way. That vision, that male fantasy of desire, presupposes a complementary fantasy of female desire. The fantasy is not "just" erotic. It is a pornographic fantasy, and so is its presentation.

As an F reader, I can resist the fantasy by exposure, by criticism, by reflection. But within the present cultural system, I do so at my own peril. I was raised and educated to comply with that male fantasy and to adopt it as my very own. Like other F readers, I may deconstruct myself at times; the temptation to reciprocate this M fantasy, even to appropriate it, may still be there. Awareness helps, but the odds are against me.[2]

[2] This inaugural lecture is a modified summary of my "The Poetics of Prophetic(?) Pornography", the last chapter in A. Brenner and F. van Dijk-Hemmes, *On Gendering Texts: Female and Male Voices in the Hebrew Bible*, Leiden, Brill, 1993.

References

Auld, G. A., "Prophecy in Books: A Rejoinder" *JSOT* 48 (1990), 31-32.

Benjamin, J., "The Bonds of Love: Rational Violence and Erotic Domination", in H. Eisenstein and A. Jardine (eds.), *The Future of Difference*, Boston: G. K. Hall, 1980, 41-70.

Benjamin, J., *The Bonds of Love*, New York, Pantheon, 1988.

Bird, P., "The Harlot as Heroine: Narrative Art and Social Presupposition in Three Old Testament Texts", *Semeia* 46 (1989a), 397-419.

Bird, P., "'To Play the Harlot': An Inquiry into an Old Testament Metaphor", in P. L. Day (ed.), *Gender and Difference in Ancient Israel*, Minneapolis, Fortress Press, 1989b, 75-94.

Caplan, P. J., *The Myth of Women's Masochism*, New York, Signet, 1987.

Carroll, R.P., *Jeremiah: A Commentary* (OTL), London, SCM Press, 1986.

——, "Whose Prophet? Whose History? Whose Social Reality? Troubling the Interpretative Community Again: Notes towards a Response to T.W. Overholt's Critique", *JSOT* 48 (1990), 33-49.

Dijk-Hemmes, F. van, "The Imagination of Power and the Power of Imagination: An Intertextual Analysis of Two Biblical Love Songs, The Song of Songs and Hosea 2", *JSOT* 44 (1989), 75-88.

——, "The Metaphorization of Woman in Prophetic Speech: An Analysis of Ezekiel 23", in A. Brenner and F. van Dijk-Hemmes, *On Gendering Texts: Female and Male voice in the Hebrew Bible*, Leiden, Brill, 1993.

Freud, S., *Jokes and their Relation to the Unconscious* (English trans.), Pelican, 1976, 1981.

Janeway, E., "Who Does What to Whom? The Psychology of the Oppressor", in A. Bach (ed.), *Ad Feminam: Union Seminary Quarterly Review* 43 (1989), 133-44.

Lloyd-Jones, H., *Female of the Species. Semonides on Women: The First Satire on Women in European Literature*, London, Duckworth, 1975.

Magonet, J., "Jeremiah's Last Confessions: Structure, Image and Ambiguity", *Hebrew Annual Review* 11 (1987), 303-17.

Overholt, T. W., "'It Is Difficult to Read'", *JSOT* 48 (1990), 51-54.

——, "Prophecy in History: The Social Reality of Intermediation", *JSOT* 48 (1990), 3-29.

Setel, D. T., "Prophets and Pornography: Female Sexual Imagery in Hosea", in L. Russell, *Feminist Interpretation of the Bible*, Philadelphia, Westminster Press, 1985, 86-95.